Stories of
Oxford Castle
From Dungeon to Dunghill

MARK DAVIES

Oxford Towpath Press

Second edition

2019

ISBN 978-0-9535593-7-4 (2nd edition)
0-9535593-3-5 (1st edition)

A catalogue record for this book is available from the British Library.

With sincere thanks for the financial contribution from
the Greening Lamborn Trust, the objective of which is
to promote public interest in the history, architecture,
old photographs, and heritage of Oxford and its
neighbourhood by supporting publications or
other media that creates access to them.

Published by

Oxford Towpath Press
12 Hythe Bridge Arm
Oxford Canal
Oxford
OX1 2TA

oxfordtowpathpress@gmail.com

www.oxfordwaterwalks.co.uk

Book design & chapter illustrations by Bryony Clark

Printed by TJ International Ltd, Padstow, Cornwall

Mrs Pauline Wilsdon
Flat 69
Fernleigh, Buttercross Lane,
Witney OX28 4DZ
Tel: 01993 771857

Contents

✦

CHAPTER EIGHT
Executions for Crimes other than Murder 171

Preface

->-<-

In December 2005, the public was allowed free access to the precincts of the former Oxford Castle for the first time in its history, as the site was converted to a hotel, restaurants, a heritage centre, and public open space, as well as some housing. The first edition of this book was timed to coincide with that moment by exposing the experiences of some of the men and women who had occasion to know the place under rather different circumstances – namely as either prisoners or as their custodians.

With the first edition long out of print – bibliophiles may like to know that 2,000 copies were printed, in two marginally different impressions – yet with no other author having attempted any comparable publication, a revision seemed in order. Naively I anticipated that it would take only a matter of weeks, simply to check some details, to refine some of the more inelegant writing, and to introduce a few new names and incidents. Several months later a halt had to be called, and while the current edition includes all of the stories which appeared in the first, they have all been revised and the whole book to some extent reordered so that the pattern of each chapter is more satisfactorily chronological.

The new edition has also been expanded by the inclusion of two new chapters. One is devoted entirely to Daniel Harris, the most influential of all the Oxford gaolers, but whose extraordinary contribution within the prison and beyond has not been widely appreciated. The other new chapter is a summary of my book *The Abingdon Waterturnpike Murder* (of which 1,600 copies were produced in two impressions). This intriguing case, in which Harris played a key role, was of especial fascination to me because of the central role played by the river bargemen and their families, a few of which had come to my attention while researching my first books, *Our Canal in Oxford* and *A Towpath Walk in Oxford*.

The three principal sources used in compiling the first edition were a) the records of the Oxfordshire quarter sessions courts stored at the Oxfordshire History Centre (OHC) in Cowley, b) Oxford's weekly newspaper, *Jackson's Oxford Journal* (first published in May 1753), and c) contemporary broadsides, pamphlets, and other publications held mainly at the OHC and the Bodleian Library, Oxford. Since then, much more information has appeared online, most helpfully a range of eighteenth-century material (Eighteenth-Century Collections Online) and the British Library's digitisation of national and local newspapers.

But it is still the manuscript material, the quarter sessions records, which were the principal starting point for most of the stories. These county magistrates' courts were held four times a year, with the Epiphany sessions in January, followed by those of Easter, Trinity, and Michaelmas at intervals of three months or so. The minute books for all the sessions from Easter 1687 to Michaelmas 1830 survive, as too do most of the original documents considered at each session. The most revealing of these are the bills submitted by various gaolers and tradesmen, appeals for clemency from impoverished prisoners, and the lists (known as Calendars) of prisoners held in the castle at the time of each session. From these documents it is possible to deduce much about the way in which the prison was run and the condition of the buildings. More revealingly, however, they also shed light on the prisoners' treatment and their backgrounds, on their attitude to authority and to each other, and on both the logic and logistics of transportation to the American colonies.

All this fascinating detail would have remained largely obscured had it not been for the extraordinary efforts of Canon William John Oldfield (1857–1934) in transcribing, indexing, and cross-indexing the 38,600 documents of which these records are comprised. He completed this immense task in September 1926. As he did so without any obvious errors, my faith in his accuracy (and indeed his ability to decipher archaic handwriting much more successfully than me!) has meant that on occasions it is Oldfield's transcriptions that I have relied on, rather than the primary source.

Throughout the book, named streets or parishes can be assumed to be in Oxford unless otherwise stated, and similarly all villages to be in Oxfordshire (bearing in mind that the River Thames historically constituted the county border, meaning that those parts of modern Oxfordshire which lie to the south or west of the river were formerly part of Berkshire, as shown in Figure 1). In quoted text, from both printed and handwritten sources, the initial capital letters used on nouns have usually been edited down. On account of the thorough indexing of both the Oxfordshire quarter sessions documents and of *Jackson's Oxford Journal*, it was not thought necessary to provide exact references for all quotations.

Acknowledgements

My main thanks go to Catherine Robinson for her immaculate editing, her advice and encouragement, and not least for her suggestion for the book's sub-title. Thanks are also due to Bryony Clark, for her further refinement of the title, as well as for her self-evident skilful design work and patience. My research was made all the more pleasant and meaningful by the ever-helpful staff of the Oxfordshire History Centre (in Cowley, Oxford), and the Special Collections staff at the Bodleian Library, Oxford. Others to whom I am grateful for their assistance or encouragement with one or both editions are Jaine Blackwell, Carl Boardman, Alison Butler, Peter and Susan Clare, Judith Curthoys, Tom Hassall, Derrick Holt, Stephanie Jenkins, Tim Metcalfe, Julian Munby, Christopher Parker, Dan Poore, and Sanders of Oxford. I am also deeply grateful to the trustees of the Greening Lamborn Trust, without whose financial support this revised edition would not have been possible.

Mark Johnstone Davies
"Bill the Lizard", Oxford,
September 2018

The Author

Mark Davies has lived on a narrowboat in central Oxford since 1992. He has published four previous books under the imprint of Oxford Towpath Press. These are *Our Canal in Oxford* (1999) and *A Towpath Walk in Oxford* (2001; 2012), both co-written with Catherine Robinson; *The Abingdon Waterturnpike Murder* (2003; 2008) and *Alice's Oxford on Foot* (2014; 2015; 2016; 2018). He is also the author of *Alice in Waterland* (2010; 2012) and *'King of all Balloons'* (2015), for which, see the end of this book.

To complement the books, Mark leads walks and gives talks for a variety of local interest groups, public institutions, and academic bodies, based on the themes of: the social history of the Oxford Canal and River Thames in Oxford, on the literary relevance of Oxford's waterways, on the Welsh associations with Oxford, and on eighteenth-century crime and punishment.

www.oxfordwaterwalks.co.uk

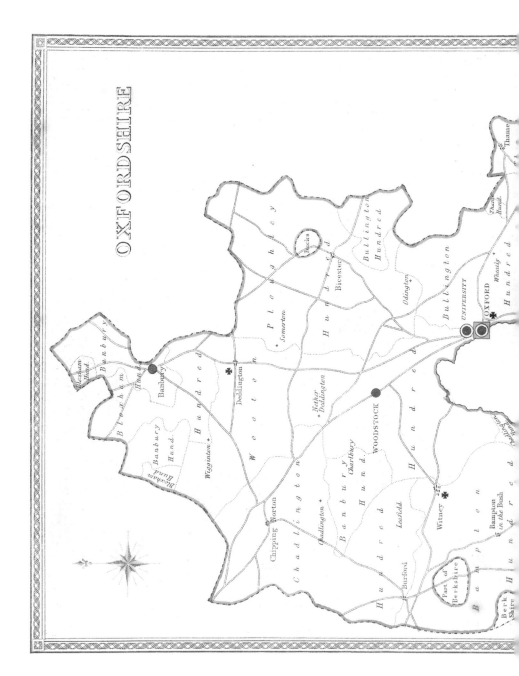

OXFORDSHIRE

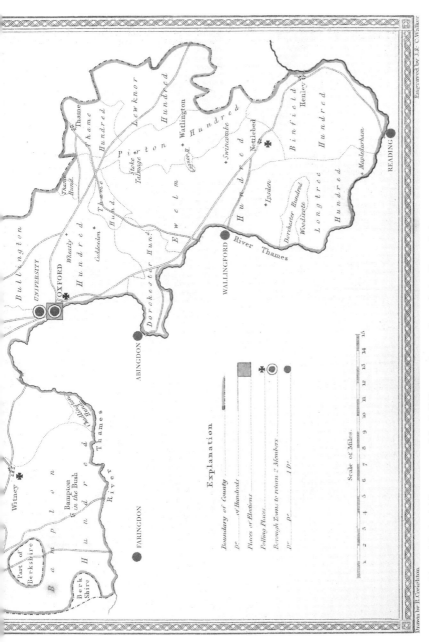

FIGURE 1 Map of Oxfordshire engraved for R.K. Dawson's 1832 *Boundaries Commission*.
The locations of Abingdon, Faringdon, Reading, and Wallingford have been added for greater clarity.

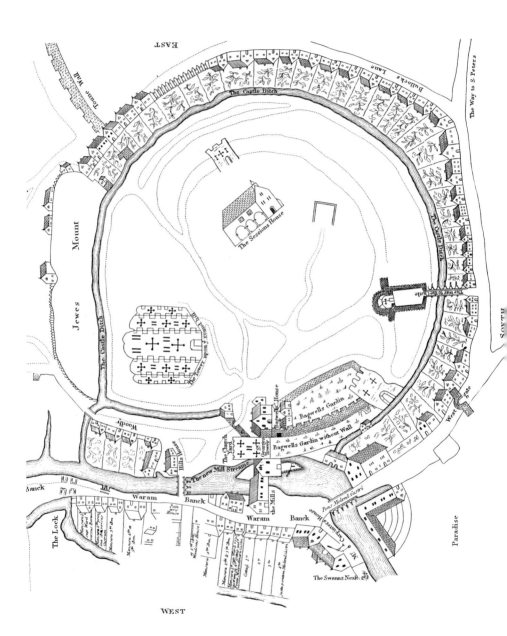

CHAPTER ONE

GAOLERS, KEEPERS, GOVERNORS, AND CUSTODIANS

By the standards of many English castles, Oxford's has had a relatively uneventful past. It has rarely been a royal residence or featured in any battles of note, and has only occasionally played a part in matters of national importance. However, its role as a county prison is a fascinating and unusual one, casting light on the lives of the ordinary – and often extraordinary – people who found themselves, however briefly, enclosed within its walls. Most of the individuals who are featured in the following chapters lived in the seventeenth and eighteenth centuries, but a brief survey of the castle's early history will help to set their situations in context.

FIGURE 2 Extract from a copy of a plan produced for Christ Church in about 1616, to clarify the boundaries of the college's purchase. Of note is "The Tower upon ye round hill", "The Sessions House" (scene of the 1577 Black Assize), with nearby gallows, and "Bullocks Lane". Next to "St. George's Tower" (with its adjacent mills) is "Bagwell's house"; this is a reference to the gaoler, Thomas Bagwell (c.1576–1631+), who also had possession of two large garden plots.

The earliest mention of Oxford occurs in the Anglo-Saxon Chronicle of 912, when the settlement was important enough to be ranked with London as a key stronghold of King Edward the Elder's defence of Wessex against the Danes. The Thames was already a well-used waterway, enabling communication between London and important towns such as Wallingford, Abingdon, and Oxford, so control of the river was of essential strategic importance. Oxford's original Saxon fort was therefore positioned to provide a vantage point over what was then the main navigable course of the Thames, called today the Castle Mill Stream (see Figures 2, 3,

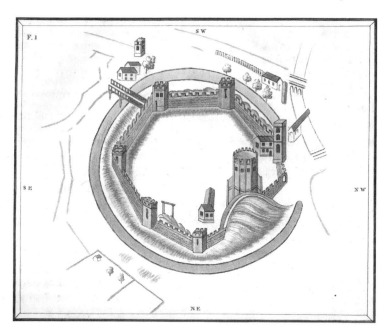

FIGURE 3 An extract from Ralph Agas' map of 1578 redrawn by the gaoler Daniel Harris, engraved for Edward King's *Vestiges of Oxford Castle* (1796). The orientation is unusual, with north east at the bottom and south west at the top, so that the Castle Mill Stream appears to the right. The main entrance to the castle is to the south, via a bridge over the moat.

and 8). Subsequently uniting with various sidestreams to the west of the town, the Thames then flowed eastwards to be joined by the Cherwell, as today. The city therefore had riverine protection on every side except the north.

The Norman castle

-+>-<+-

After the Norman Conquest, the existing Saxon fortress was strengthened by Robert d'Oyley (or d'Oilly), who was appointed by King William as its custodian. D'Oyley constructed a stone keep on top of the motte, probably replacing an existing wooden structure, and by 1071 had completed a high outer wall of stone incorporating six defensive towers with a surrounding moat (see Figure 3). Only the tower of St George remains, preserved on account of its special importance as protection for the adjacent mill from which the name Castle Mill Stream derives.

The keep constituted a powerful symbol of Norman dominance, visible to the whole neighbourhood. The local population submitted unwillingly to d'Oyley's stringent methods, and it seems likely that almost immediately the castle would have doubled as a prison for the most persistently unwilling. However, it was not until early in the reign of Henry III, who acceded in 1216, that a portion of the castle was specifically designated as a prison,* expressly for the incarceration of rebellious clerks from the University.† At about the

---

* The term prison came into common usage only after a statute of 1865 decreed that "the distinct titles of Gaol and House of Correction are merged into the appellative of Prison", therefore "gaol" is the word more usually used in this book.

† The earliest known story about Oxford Castle is a thirteenth-century romance, *Blonde of Oxford and Jehan of Dammartin*, in which the castle is portrayed as the home of the Earl of Oxford.

same time it became the common gaol for the county, and housed the shire and assize courts until the eventful Black Assize of 1577 (see Chapter 5).

Deemed superfluous by the Crown, the site was purchased by two "gentlemen of London", Francis James and Robert Younglove, who sold it on to Christ Church in 1613. A plan from about this time (see Figure 2) shows that domestic houses, each with its own garden plot, had encroached on the moat, indicative of the castle's lack of military importance. The prison consisted at this time of a small cluster of buildings next to St George's Tower. These included the home of the keeper of the gaol, probably Thomas Bagwell (c.1576–?), successor to John Bagwell, who was buried at St Thomas' Church on 13 July 1605. Little is known about the Bagwells, but Thomas was summoned for a somewhat curious misdemeanour in 1622, being charged at the Michaelmas quarter sessions with making "saucy and rash comparisons between his wife and the best wives in the town. He admitted the same penitently, asked the favour of the court", and was discharged.

Following the purchase by Christ Church, the site was leased to the county, which appointed a gaoler to oversee and operate the establishment as a kind of franchised business. It is a tangible example of the power of the University in Oxford that the county magistrates should be so beholden to a single college for the best part of the next two centuries. The University had its own courts and system of justice, so it was only very rarely that any students found themselves contemplating the insides of the castle as anything other than visitors.

Cyril Wilsdon is buried here ←

"Inhumane, unspeakable, and unheard-of usage": the Civil War

-+->-<+-

The castle assumed brief military importance during the Civil War, when Oxford was at the centre of the Royalist cause for nearly four years, from the day when Charles I entered Oxford in October 1642 to his surrender to Oliver Cromwell's Parliamentarians in June 1646. The earliest first-hand accounts of conditions for prisoners appear at about this time – a time, indeed, when the most inoffensive of men could find themselves behind bars, with the most inappropriate of men in charge of them! Several accounts survive of the especially brutal regime at Oxford imposed by two men called Smith: Thomas and William.

A clergyman called Edward Wirley was held in the castle at the end of 1642, along with numerous other men suspected of opposing the Royalist cause. In *The Prisoners' Report*, printed on the authority of the House of Commons on 20 March 1643, Wirley identified William Smith as his principal persecutor.* The prisoners were categorised as either ministers of religion (like Wirley himself), gentlemen, or common soldiers. Held in cramped, insanitary conditions, Wirley wrote that the only relief was that some gentlemen "had their libertie sometimes to walk in the castle court (a little stinking yard and the onely place that the prisoners had to ease nature, Smith not permitting any, no not with a keeper, to go to any other upon that necessitie)".

One of these gentlemen, unnamed for reasons of self-preservation,

---

* It might be assumed from the similarities of their vindictive behaviour that Thomas Smith and William Smith were one and the same man, but Wirley makes it clear that this was not the case, nor apparently were they related.

identified the other Smith, Thomas, "Marshall General", as his own oppressor in a letter printed in London on 13 January 1643. In "a true relation of the most woeful and miserable state and condition of these distressed prisoners taken by his Majesties forces, and detained and kept in the castle at Oxford", he cursed Thomas Smith without restraint as "a man composed of naught but wickedness, begot by an Incubus, nursed by a Succubus, or else the very spawne of Cerberus, more fitter for the gaoler of Devills than a keeper of Christians". As examples of Smith's "inhumane, unspeakable, and unheard-of usage" he stated:

> We endure cold, hunger, and nakednesse, fetters, bolts, and irons. Our beds we lie on are stuft with feathers longer than our arms and coverlets wanting, and the hard boards our bedsteads… We are so thrust and packed up together, and in such close and small roomes, that wanting roome for us to lie, some of us are inforced perforce to stand in woeful manner until the residue take their unquiet rest.

Edmund Chillenden was another victim. After escaping in 1643, he printed his own account,* stating:

> I doe believe, that the barbariousnes inflicted upon the poore gally slaves in Turky, cannot parallell those inhumane cruelties, which abundance of poore men have undergon from the hands of Smith himselfe.

These men, the common soldiers, included 180 Republican survivors of the defeat at Marlborough. According to Edward Wirley, in December 1642 they were all "put up in to an high tower, and lodged upon the boards: the rooms were so stuffed with them that

---

* *The inhumanity of the Kings prison-keeper at Oxford, Or a true relation of the most transcendent cruelties, cheatings, cozenings, and base dishonest dealings of William Smith*, 1643.

they could not lie downe one by another". As a clergyman, Wirley was allowed special access to these men, but by the same measure exposed himself to accusations of spreading dissent. William Smith had Wirley beaten on this pretext, and paraded him through the town on market day, en route to incarceration in the dungeon of the city bridewell, known as the Bocardo.*

Conditions in the Bocardo were still more intolerable. Many of the inmates had been captured after the Royalist victory at Cirencester in February 1643, and it was so crowded that Wirley had to sit upright at night for the next three weeks, at the bottom of the stairs to the dungeon. This was comparative luxury, because on the floor itself "in some places of it a man might have gon almost over his shoes in pisse" because

> we had no place for the easement of nature but that where wee were in, both night and day. Also sick persons were forced in the same place to empty their stomacks, so that the stinch of the place was enough to poyson us.

When they protested, William Smith replied that "they should have nothing but bread and water, and if in case they dyed, should be cast on a dunghill". Smith's vindictive nature is underlined by the way that he ordered the keeper of the Bocardo to be thrown into his own dungeon for showing too much compassion to the men under his charge. This man's name was probably Giles Carter, who later died "in great extremity" at the castle, where he was identified by Edmund Chillenden as the "man that dwelt in the Bridewell".

---

* The bridewell or city gaol (called the Bocardo by at least 1391) stood at the North Gate near St Michael's Church, and was intended mainly for holding local residents accused of relatively minor misdemeanours. The Bocardo's most famous prisoners, however, were the Protestant bishops Thomas Cranmer, Nicholas Ridley, and Hugh Latimer, who were held there before their executions in 1555 and 1556.

John Taylor the Waterpoet

It was at this time that one of the most colourful and resilient of all the men caught up in the turmoil of the Civil War arrived in Oxford from London. His name was John Taylor (1578–1653), a royal waterman. A great traveller, among the many long and often intrepid journeys about which Taylor "the Waterpoet" published humorous accounts was the first-ever survey of the entire River Thames (in 1632). In a collection of siege papers at the Bodleian Library is one dated 22 May 1643 which refers to "the water bayly and Mr. Jo. Taylor – employed to give information of the boats and boatmen" and states that "there be a stopp that none pass without a ticket of the Commission and all boats to be searched". Taylor's hydrological and boating knowledge was of great value to the besieged city, but it was his skill with the pen which gives him particular historical significance. While in Oxford he published numerous pamphlets in support of the Royalist cause, aiming light-hearted poetical salvos at the Roundhead opposition. In *Mad Verse, Sad Verse, Glad Verse, and Bad Verse*, published in Oxford in May 1644, he wrote:

> I was commanded by the Water Baylie
> To see the River clensed, both night and dayly
> Dead Hogges, Dogges, Cats and well flayed Carryon Horses
> Their noysom Corpses soyld the water courses.

Taylor's solution was to utilise a convenient labour force, the captured prisoners:

> And now and then was punish a Deliquent,
> By which good means away the filth and stink went.

The later seventeenth century: the Thorpe family

+>-<+-

Whether conditions at Oxford Castle improved much during the Puritan Commonwealth is unknown. Following Sir Thomas Glenham's surrender of the castle to Thomas Fairfax on 24 June 1646, the next three provosts are named in John M. Davenport's pamphlet, *Notes as to Oxford Castle** as Thomas Keylsley in 1648; and Colonel Richard Ingoldsby and Lieutenant Colonel Kessey in 1649. Ingoldsby (1617–1685) was one of the regicides who signed Charles I's death warrant, yet was knighted by Charles II at his coronation in 1660. Of especial local note, it was Ingoldsby who ordered the demolition of five of the castle's six Norman towers, which, as Davenport wrote, "had added strength and beauty to the castle; but, on the other hand, he constructed costly bulwarks for greater security".

These new works were short-lived, however. Despite having taken more than a year to build, at considerable cost, in 1652 they were "in four dayes' space in a whimsey quite pulled down and demolished", according to the Oxford diarist and historian, Anthony Wood. From then on, the castle became exclusively the common gaol for the county, with the governor or keeper appointed by the sheriff. The site was still owned by Christ Church, and the system of leasing the buildings to individuals who received no salary, but ran the prison as a business, was resumed. It was this arrangement which pertained in 1687, when the earliest surviving records of the

---

* Davenport was the Clerk of the Peace of Oxfordshire County Council, and stated at the time (1877) that he had searched extensively for the names of more governors, but had been constrained because "there are no old records whatever in the Prison".

Oxfordshire quarter sessions (held at the Oxfordshire History Centre at Cowley) begin to reveal the story of the castle and its temporary residents in more consistent detail.

The gaoler at this time was, intriguingly, and probably for the first time, a woman. Mrs Elizabeth Thorpe (?–1696) seems to have succeeded to the role after her husband, Robert (1636?–1679). Her name appears in documents dated between 1685 and 1691, after which it is again a male member of the family who is referenced.* Elizabeth Thorpe seems to have upheld the sadistic standards set by the Smiths in the 1640s, if a letter by Thomas Hill, published in Moses Pitt's *The Cry of the Oppressed* in 1691, is any indication. His account is interesting not so much because of the light that it shines on the appalling conditions endured even by men guilty of no greater offence than debt, but because of the significantly powerful positions held by women at this particular moment.

Hill was a debtor, and he recounted how one evening he had "sent a woman, who is a messenger to the prison, for provision my friends had sent me". When the woman failed to return, Hill denounced her to some fellow debtors, calling her, among other things, "an old bitch". The comment was unfortunately overheard by the nurse, "a Devilish woman, who has always been malitious [sic] to me". Subsequently "Mistress Thorp, the prison-keeper came to me, and caused me to have irons, and a great piece of wood, as big as any mans thigh, to be lock'd about my leg". Hill concluded that "a man would better be subject to slavery than to this woman,

---

* Robert Thorp and Elizabeth Porson or Pecson married at St Thomas' on 17 March 1667. The couple had six children baptised there between 1669 and 1679, Robert dying that same year (deduced because at her own burial on 14 January 1696 she was described as a widow). It would seem that one of their sons – logically the eldest, Robert (c.1667–1697?), stood in briefly as gaoler after his mother's death. Another son, William (baptised in 1670), became a student at New College.

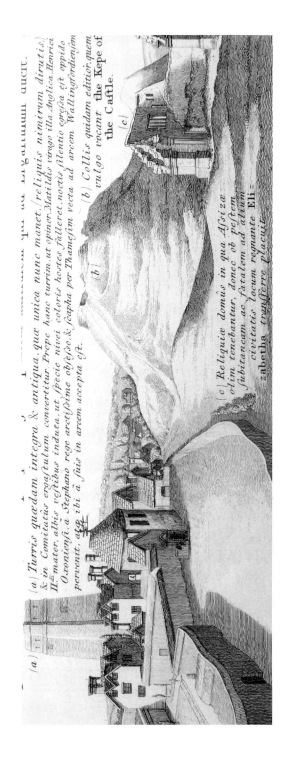

FIGURE 4 "Remains of Oxford Castle" as drawn in 1719 by Michael Burghers, and reproduced by John Skelton in 1820. St George's Tower (a), the keeper's house (at the time occupied by the Ettys), and Horde's chapel are clearly depicted, and to the right (c) are the ruins of the court building in which the assizes were held until 1577.

for she is a Devil", seeming to imply that he thought that penal transportation would be preferable to continued incarceration. If so, it was a sentiment which others would have shared at this time (see Chapter 4).

The Etty family
➤>‹‹-

In 1699 comes the first appearance in the quarter sessions documentation of the name Etty, an Abingdon family who governed the castle prison for the next four decades, and retained a leasehold interest in the site for twice that time. Andrew Etty (?–c.1718) was the first incumbent. Noted as both a barber and an innkeeper while in Abingdon, he and his wife Jane had six children baptised between 1684 and 1689 before he moved to Oxford to take up the role of gaoler. On Andrew's death, his brother Richard (1660–?), an important bargemaster on the Thames – as too was Richard's son Francis (1699–1753) – acquired the lease of both the castle and its chapel, jointly with Walter Lardner, a Bampton grocer. The role of governor, however, was assumed by Andrew's son, Marmaduke (c.1685–?), who is referred to in documentation between 1720 and 1730, and he in turn was succeeded by Mrs Elizabeth Etty, his presumed wife (and the daughter of Walter Lardner), from 1732 to 1740. The couple had five children baptised at St Thomas' Church between 1714 and 1730.* The last of the family to oversee the castle prison was Charles Etty (from 1739 to 1742), possibly Marmaduke's older brother (who had been baptised in Abingdon in 1684). The

---

* There is a gap of ten years between the baptisms of the third and fourth children, in 1716 and 1726, during which period another son, James, was born, in about 1724 – see Chapter 2.

Ettys continued to retain leasehold interest in parts of the site until the transfer of the site to the county in the 1780s, however.*

The transition from the Ettys to the next gaoling dynasty, the Wisdom family, is encapsulated in a letter written by two debtors, whose typically long periods of incarceration gave them ample opportunity to observe the minutiae of the prison's internal changes. Writing in January 1742, their request was for glass to be installed in the window of the debtors' cell. The authors pointed to a precedent of January 1739, when the debtors "then lying in the tower or common side" had successfully requested that an open window should be glazed. When the number of debtors had increased in the previous November, Mr Etty, "the late keeper", had been obliged to lodge some of them in a second room. Mr Wisdom, "the current keeper", was continuing to hold debtors in this room, but it too had "a window without any glass on the north east side … which is at least fifty feet high whereby your petitioners who lodge in the same room are very much exposed to the inclemency of the weather to the impairing of their healths". This deferential, articulate (and successful) request contains the earliest reference to the Wisdoms, the family who would run the prison for nearly the next half century.

---

* Davenport's (admittedly patchy) list places Charles Etty as gaoler from 1717 until at least 1741. Conceivably, different members of the family undertook the role on an interchangeable basis, according to availability, health, and so on. In Oxford, that clearly included the widows of incumbent gaolers. Female keepers of male prisons were prohibited by law in 1782.

FIGURE 5 *Oxford Castle in Oxfordshire.* A 1785 print published by Alexander Hogg, based on a 1751 view drawn by Francis Grose in his *Antiquities of England & Wales*. The chapel (founded by Thomas Horde) is in the centre, with the gallows nearby to the right. John Howard's observation that "the gaoler has a spacious garden" is beyond dispute!

William Wisdom (c.1704–1769):
gaoler from 1742 to 1769

-+>-<+-

William Wisdom was presumably the man of that name who acquired his freedom of the city (that is, the right to trade on his own behalf within the liberty of Oxford) on 14 January 1733. His likely father Henry – appropriately enough, in view of William's own subsequent career – had been a locksmith. It was during William Wisdom's long tenure as gaoler that the first issue of *Jackson's Oxford Journal* appeared, in May 1753, providing for the first time some consistent additional insights into the workings of the prison. *Jackson's* appears to have meticulously recorded all the escapes and executions of prisoners (as will be seen in the following chapters), and the fact that the newspaper reported no escapes at all during William Wisdom's time suggests that he performed his duties efficiently. All in all, it is probably indicative of a well-run operation that the only time that William Wisdom's name was brought to the attention of *Jackson's* readers was when he died, in June 1769, at the age of 63.* Poignantly, William's widow, Ann, died exactly a week later, after suffering "a paralitick stroke". In his 1767 will, Wisdom had left his entire estate to his wife. Because she died so soon after him, the legacy passed to Susanna (wife of John) Lambourn, the sole executrix of Ann, although there is no obvious family connection.† Nor indeed is the inter-relationship

---

* This was the age stated in his obituary, although it is presumably his baptism that was recorded at All Saints in 1704, and presumably those of his children in 1734 and 1735. His subsequent children were baptised at St Thomas', the first being Richard on 14 April 1742, which corresponds with William's assumption of the role of gaoler the year before. Two more children followed: Aaron (1744) and Moses (1746).

† William was buried at St Ebbe's on 22 June 1769, and Ann on the 28th.

clear between Charles, who succeeded William, nor yet Solomon, the third Wisdom to hold the position. It is possible that Charles was the son of William Wisdom, perukemaker, who gained his freedom in 1768: the timing, a year before he became gaoler, may be pertinent, but the relationship is by no means certain.

Charles Wisdom: gaoler from 1769 to 1774

-+>-<+-

Conditions inside the gaol seem to have deteriorated during Charles Wisdom's tenure, despite his early reassurances to the contrary. Within months of his appointment, it was felt necessary to advise an anxious public that rumours of an outbreak of gaol distemper were false. *Jackson's* of 30 September 1769 reported that, while it was true that two prisoners had recently died, "both of them were aged persons, sinking under complicated diseases".* The newspaper went on to comment (with perhaps suspicious hyperbole):

> The rest of the prisoners, as well as Mr Wisdom's family, are now, and have been, in as perfect a state of health as can at any time be remembered, as are also the inhabitants of this city in general.

Be that as it might, outbreaks of gaol fever and smallpox became commonplace thereafter, such that eleven prisoners died of smallpox in 1773 alone (see Figure 18). A contributing factor may have been the additional requirement to accommodate prisoners from the Bocardo when it was demolished in 1771. This arrangement continued until a new city prison was opened at Gloucester Green

---

* One may have been Hannah Cripps, buried at St Thomas' Church on 13 September – see Chapter 4.

in 1789. In such confined quarters, contagion was inevitable, and perhaps it was the incentivising threat of this more immediate and fatal termination of their sentences as much as the gradual deterioration of the buildings that led to a succession of escapes from this point on. Notices relating to two such "enlargements" within the space of two months (see Chapter 3) – in September and November 1774 – mark the transition from Charles Wisdom to the third of the family to hold the post of keeper.

Solomon Wisdom (c.1726–1809): gaoler from 1774 to 1786

→>-<←

From available sources it would seem that little was amiss at Oxford Castle Gaol during the tenure of the first two Wisdoms. There is no hint of bad treatment (indeed, rather the opposite is suggested by the consistently high cost to the county of providing food and medical treatment for poor prisoners), and it appears that justice was carried out in as orderly and civilised a manner as the standards of the time would allow.

Things were a lot less settled during the governorship of Solomon Wisdom, however. This was not necessarily a reflection on Wisdom himself. There is some evidence towards the end of his tenure that he might have abused his position, but external factors conspired to make his role probably far more challenging than any other in that century. Previously, felons had been held until their cases were tried, at either the March or the July assizes each year, and those found guilty of non-capital crimes would then often be removed as transports destined for America. In 1776, however, that destination ceased to be a viable option as Britain's war with America intensified.

As a result, overcrowding exacerbated the already daunting aspects of incarceration. The end of the war in 1783 only made matters worse, as a lack of employment for returning troops led almost inevitably to an increase in crime. By March 1784, for instance, there were 49 male felons in the castle, plus an indeterminate number of debtors, when the previous prison population had been typically less than half that.

This was a situation with national implications, and while Solomon Wisdom was gaoler he received many visits from the influential prison reformer, John Howard (1726–1790). Howard had been Sheriff of Bedfordshire until 1773. He had therefore been able to observe at first hand the plight of prisoners, who endured conditions of great deprivation and intimidation on account of the policy of denying gaolers any consistent means of support other than the fees paid by the prisoners themselves. Howard therefore advocated that gaolers should be paid a salary, and he visited numerous prisons between 1773 and 1775 to see if there was any precedent for this. In so doing, he discovered "scenes of calamity which I grew daily more and more anxious to alleviate". These he recorded in *The State of the Prisons in England and Wales* (first published in 1777), in which he reproduced the (unattributed) observations of Dr Samuel Johnson (first published in *The Idler* of 6 January 1759) as an encapsulation of his own opinion (slightly amended in the third edition of 1784):

> The misery suffered in gaols is not half their evil; they are filled with every sort of corruption that poverty and wickedness can generate: with all the shameless and profligate enormities that can be produced by the impudence of ignominy, the rage of want, and the malignity of despair. In a prison the check of the public eye is

removed; and the power of the law is spent. There are few fears, there are no blushes. The lewd inflame the more modest; the audacious harden the timid. Every one fortifies himself as he can against his own remaining sensibility, endeavouring to practise on others the arts that are practised on himself, and to gain the applause of his worst associates by imitating their manners.

At Oxford, Howard noted in 1780 that the courtyard used by prisoners of both sexes measured only 29 by 23 feet; the "felons' day-room or hall for *men and women*" was 12 by 15 feet; the men's dungeon (measuring 18½ by 16½ feet in 1782) had only "small apertures"; and "the women's night-room 6½ feet by 4 feet; no windows". So, there was very little space at a time when prisoners could expect long periods of confinement and a surplus of company. Describing the interiors, Howard wrote: "No infirmary: no bath: no straws: the prisoners lie in their clothes on mats. The men's dungeon swarms with vermin; yet not white-washed for many years". His final comment was a surely pointed rebuke: "The gaoler has a spacious garden."

Well, to be fair, the gaoler probably needed it! It should not be forgotten that in some respects the keepers were as trapped as their charges. As they lived in close proximity to large numbers of often desperate and potentially or actually violent men and women, who endured conditions of varying degrees of deprivation and squalor, it is fair to say that it was not a job for the faint-hearted! There is no evidence that any of the Oxford keepers were actually assaulted, but the fear must always have been present. When *Jackson's* noted on 28 February 1784 the foiled plan of 27 felons to seize Solomon Wisdom at locking-up time, this was doubtless not the only such occurrence. Nor probably was the incident to which John Howard

FIGURE 6 *St Thomas' Church* from James Ingram's 1837 *Memorials of Oxford*. As the church most closely associated with the castle, St Thomas' has seen the burials of many terminally ill or executed criminals as well as some of the custodians who were responsible for those executions.

referred during his visit in December 1782: "the felons' day-room is paved with flat stones, in consequence of their taking up the pebbles for defence, after an attempt to escape".

Heeding Howard's recommendations, the Oxfordshire magistrates conceded the need for the role of governor to become a salaried post, and as from 24 June 1784 Wisdom was paid a wage of £50 a year, mainly, as it was stated, in lieu of the obviously lucrative former right "of selling ale and liquor". Another major change soon followed. If political factors meant that Solomon Wisdom faced more severe tests in the science of incarceration than either of his family predecessors, another factor was more straightforward: the deterioration of the prison's physical structure. Throughout the century, the Oxfordshire magistrates had regularly paid masons, smiths, carpenters, and others for repairs, at considerable cumulative cost. Eventually the fundamental problem had to be faced: only a complete redevelopment would solve all the difficulties. To achieve this, however, the county concluded that complete control of the site was needed, and purchase negotiations commenced with Christ Church.

The sequence of change can be traced from the notices placed in *Jackson's*. The earliest appears on 16 October 1784, when the newspaper advised that the "insufficiency and want of repairs at the castle gaol" would be considered at the next quarter sessions. Sure enough, the magistrates' minutes for Epiphany 1785 contain a resolution to undertake wholesale reconstruction of the site. To do so, the county paid £331 10s to Christ Church and a further £800 in respect of the various leases (held on 40-year terms) "vested in Charles Etty Esq. and others under the several wills of the Rev. Andrew Etty and James Etty deceased" (see Chapter 2).

In *Jackson's* of 9 April 1785 the new designs of the London architect William Blackburn were made public, with an invitation to builders and masons to tender "for making a boundary wall round the castle gaol at Oxford, and a wing to the intended bridewell to be built within the said wall". The city too was active at this time. As stated above, city prisoners had been held at the castle ever since the demolition of the old Bocardo in 1771. Now tenders were also invited (*Jackson's* 16 July 1785) to build "a boundary wall and gaol, and a house of correction in Gloucester Green".

The following year, Blackburn's designs for the castle prison were under way. On 8 April 1786 there was an invitation in *Jackson's* for tenders "for building one wing of the intended gaol and house of correction and the carcase of the keeper's house". This notice is of especial interest in that it advises that particulars could be obtained from the Clerk of Works at the castle. Although not named, the post-holder was Daniel Harris, who was destined to succeed Solomon Wisdom as keeper, and would go on to have an influence of enormous and lasting consequence, not merely within the confines of the prison, but throughout the city and beyond.

CHAPTER TWO

DANIEL 'DAMNABLE' HARRIS
(1761?–1840)
Gaoler, Builder, Engineer, Artist, and Architect

The appointment of Daniel Harris marked a new breed of prison governor. The days of family dynasties such as the Thorpes, Ettys, and Wisdoms having passed, Harris was a more accountable public servant, paid a handsome salary more than double that of Solomon Wisdom's short-lived pay. In return, he was required to exhibit a concomitant professionalism. This Harris appears to have done with aplomb – although there are occasional hints that his mind was not always fully on the job, or at least not on the job for which he was ostensibly paid. This was, overall, a small price to pay for employing a man of such wide-ranging talents, as Harris contrived to combine his principal custodial role with involvement in a bewildering array of construction, engineering, and artistic projects throughout the county. His introduction to public scrutiny was especially inauspicious, however, giving no hint of the enormous achievements to come.

FIGURE 7 *Daniel Damnable Surveying the Dunghill.* The insulting caricature which the prisoner David Gadsdon was obliged by Solomon Wisdom to draw in 1786. The words "cock of this dunghill" constitute an additional slight, a "dunghill cock" being a derogatory term applied to men lacking in spirit or courage. Additionally, "to die dunghill" was a cant expression meaning "to repent, or shew any signs of contrition, at the gallows" (Francis Grose's 1785 *The Vulgar Tongue*). [*Copyright: Oxfordshire History Centre*]

Clerk of Works (1785–1786)

→>-<+-

There are no known images or descriptions of any of the civilian Oxford gaolers of the eighteenth or earlier centuries. Harris is the first for whom we have any visual clues, but even they come in a less than convincing form: an unflattering caricature drawn by a prisoner at the instigation of Harris' soon-to-be predecessor, Solomon Wisdom (see Figure 7).

The drawing, showing Harris standing on top of a small mound with the enthusiastic approval of the Devil, is entitled "Daniel Damnable surveying the Dunghill". The dunghill in question, as revealed by two documents presented at the Michaelmas 1786 quarter sessions, was a source of dispute. Wisdom had twice allowed some of the debtors to relocate part of this pile of earth and rubbish within the debtors' yard, even though he had been ordered by the magistrates to ensure that it remained untouched. When Harris, as Clerk of Works, reported that this relocated material had "stopped up some drains which were made to carry off water from the foundation of the boundary wall", he was instructed by the magistrates to prevent the removal of any more material. Wisdom, resentful that this youthful newcomer should be more trusted than himself, sought some means of revenge, and decided on ridicule as his best weapon.

Aware of the artistic talents of a debtor called David Gadsdon, Wisdom coerced him into representing Harris in "a ridiculous situation and to expose him to the contempt of the debtors and the convicts". Gadsdon dared not refuse, as revealed in his letter of 21 October 1786 to the magistrates Rev. John Cooke and Christopher Willoughby. His compliance came down to a fear of reprisals, Gadsdon reminding them of the maltreatment Wisdom had inflicted on him two years previously, even though this had remained unproven because of "the false accusations and aspersions exhibited against me by the keeper". So, the drawing was duly produced, much to Wisdom's satisfaction, and pinned prominently at the entrance to prison, where as many people as possible might share the joke, to the irrecoverable detriment of Harris' reputation. Or so Wisdom hoped. Unfortunately for him, Gadsdon's confession had the opposite effect. Wisdom was dismissed by the sheriff, who concurred that his behaviour had been "contrary to the peace and good government" of the gaol. More chastening still, Harris was promoted in his place – with a hefty increase in salary to boot! But time had been running out for Solomon Wisdom in any case. His intransigence over the dunghill was not the only example of behaviour "repugnant to every plan of reform lately introduced by the magistrates", and the incident is a literally graphic demonstration of the changing times. The absolute power of the keeper over the prisoners in his charge was passing. Now prison governors were required to do exactly that: govern, with a view to helping prisoners to reform, rather than simply to guard them until such time as their punishments were decided. Daniel Harris' appointment was unanimously confirmed in January 1787.

So Daniel Harris, not yet 30 years old, found himself suddenly in a position of great responsibility at a time of enormous change. There is little doubt that he was exactly the right man for the job. Nothing is known of his early life, but it was noted in a 1793 House of Commons report on "the amendment and improvement of the navigation of the Thames and Isis" that it was as a journeyman carpenter that he had first arrived in Oxford. This was evidently the practical skill which had qualified him for the position of

Clerk of Works, and made him the ideal individual to oversee the completion of William Blackburn's designs for a radically rebuilt prison. There was change afoot elsewhere in Oxford too, however, and Harris was soon also in demand from other authorities with pressing construction needs.

Harris and the River Thames (1788–1798)

The 1793 House of Commons report into the River Thames identifies Harris as having overseen major improvements on the river in the Oxford area between 1788 and 1791. The stimulus was the additional waterborne traffic which passed to and through Oxford on completion of both the Thames and Severn Canal, which joined the Thames some 30 miles upstream near Lechlade in 1789, and of the Oxford Canal, which created the shortest water route between London and the rapidly industrialising Midlands when its Oxford terminus was opened on 1 January 1790. Oxford, renowned for centuries as an exclusive centre of cloistered learning, found itself suddenly at the centre of a national transport revolution. It was to the city's great good fortune that there was a man like Daniel Harris – resourceful, adaptable, and energetic – conveniently placed to rise to the challenge.

A crucial structure was the lock at Osney, this being both the first river lock encountered by Midlands canal traffic onward-bound towards London, but also the contrivance by which the depth of the Thames as it passed the upstream shallows of Port Meadow could be maintained. Harris' first major role on the river was to arrange the labour to see this pivotal facility completed, the Thames Commissioners authorising on 9 October 1789 a payment of £50 "to Mr. Harris the keeper of the Castle at Oxford on account of work done by the felons".

Here was the key to Harris' many subsequent employments on both the river and canal. Not only was he able to design or advise on structures such as locks, bridges, towpaths, and weirs, he could also reliably provide cheap labour to see the work through to completion. Harris completed Osney Lock in 1790; Godstow Lock, at the entrance to Port Meadow, in the same year; and in 1791 the lock at Pinkhill, a further five miles upstream.

Nonetheless, Harris was not without his detractors. Unsurprisingly, perhaps, when men who had spent years training to become professional surveyors and engineers were asked to inspect his work they sometimes found fault, although it is impossible to know if this was born of truly impartial professionalism or simple spite. The Scot Robert Mylne (best known for his design of Blackfriars Bridge in London) was especially critical. In 1791 he inspected the stretch of river for which Harris had been given responsibility, from Godstow to Abingdon. Afterwards, Harris confided in aggrieved tones to one of the Thames Commissioners with whom he was especially familiar, the magistrate Christopher Willoughby,* that Mylne's "conversation with me was principally to let me know his own extraordinary ability and experience, and my want thereof". This was followed a little later by the publication of a pamphlet in which Mylne included the opinion, laden with irony, that "the Thames must flourish while Mr. Harris, the Oxford Gaoler, is employed as an extra official engineer". This was not the only

---

* It is thanks to Willoughby that Gadsdon's drawing of Harris – the only likeness known – has survived, and likewise much of the evidence concerning the 1787 "Waterturnpike Murder" (see Chapter 7). These documents had been retained by him among his private papers, now held at the Oxfordshire History Centre.

example of an appointment which Fred Thacker, in his authoritative and comprehensive book, *The Thames Highway*, described as having "brought much sarcasm on the heads of the Commissioners". Yet they stuck with Harris, at least for a few years, and a report that he submitted to Willoughby in 1794 shows the huge range of improvements and repairs that he had undertaken along almost 30 miles of river, from Rushey (near Bampton), 22 miles above Oxford, to Nuneham (see Figure 1).

Harris and the Oxford Canal (1791–1801)

-+->-<+-

If the Thames Commissioners were not dissuaded by public criticism of their choice of engineer, nor were the men responsible for the new Oxford Canal, although it was Harris' architectural and building skills that initially caught their attention.

Construction of the Oxford Canal had commenced near Coventry in 1769. It took twenty years to complete to Oxford, and – after two major injections of extra capital during construction – was an immediate success. It therefore became a priority to build a warehouse on the Oxford wharf. With both Harris and his prisoners only a matter of minutes away, he was a very convenient choice of contractor, although not an obvious one, in view of his lack of any previous experience. He was therefore first requested by the canal's proprietors "to go to Birmingham and Stourport and survey the warehouses on the wharfs there" in order to assess "the most proper method of erecting warehouses on the Oxford wharf". That was on 15 October 1791, and it would seem that he wasted no time, because only four days later came the resolution that "a warehouse be erected at the east end of the basin", 80 feet by 34 feet, "and that Mr. Harris of the Castle in Oxford be requested to provide materials on the best terms and superintend the building of the same".

The work was clearly satisfactory, since in the year after its completion Harris was engaged by the Company to build a second warehouse. On 9 September 1795 it was agreed that "a warehouse according to the plan drawn by Mr. Daniel Harris be built … at the north entrance to the new wharf". However, there appears to have been a change of mind, as plans of the site at this time show no such building, and on 8 June the following year came a decision to build this second warehouse on the western side. This time, although it was to be "under the direction of Mr. Daniel Harris", it was not his own design which was used. Nonetheless, the Company *was* content to accept his plans for both an important lock and for their own new headquarters.

The lock had been discussed for some years. The original lock by which vessels could move between the Oxford Canal and the River Thames had only a single gate, and was clearly inadequate. As early as September 1792 the need for a new one had been minuted "for the purpose of admitting boats into the basin from the River without sustaining the injuries which have been repeatedly experienced from letting water out of the Basin". It was Harris to whom the Company entrusted this task, and construction was well under way by the beginning of 1795, with the final settlement of his account being made on 25 March 1797. It would seem that Harris was being paid personally for some services, since the accounts published by the county (see, for example, Figure 17) record receipts for the provision of convict labour which are smaller than the sums that the Company paid to Harris himself over the period. Today the lock is known as Isis Lock, and is one of Oxford's hidden gems, a structure of both beauty and utility in a tree-lined setting which belies its city-centre location. Harris' original design has been narrowed – at the time, his lock was required to admit Thames barges on to the canal, and so was twice the width that it is today – but it still performs an identical function, of allowing boats the same access and egress that they have enjoyed for well over two centuries.*

During this same period, Harris had also been engaged in the design and construction of the Oxford Canal Company's new, prestigious office building in New Inn Hall Lane. On 9 September 1795 – at the same meeting at which Harris' plan for a second warehouse was approved – it was agreed that "a house and offices for the use of the clerk accountant with a room for the meetings of the committee according to the plan given by Mr. Daniel Harris be built under the direction of the said Mr. Harris and that he do immediately prepare the proper materials for the same". This was to be constructed on land which had been purchased earlier that year when it came up for auction following the death of the newspaper proprietor William Jackson (see Appendix 5). Having secured the land, the Company immediately resold the two houses on the site which were surplus to their requirements, and Daniel Harris took the opportunity to secure one of them, then in the occupation of Mrs Mary Stewart or Stuart.† The transaction was completed on 25 March 1797, with a payment by Harris of £550 – a huge sum, indicative of his rapid increase in prosperity. Meanwhile,

---

* For a fuller account of Isis Lock, also known as Louse Lock, see Davies & Robinson, *A Towpath Walk in Oxford.*

† Nothing is known about Mrs Stewart; but the occupant of the other house, Elizabeth Etty (?–1800), was the widow of a wine merchant, James Etty (c.1724–1783), the son of Marmaduke Etty, the former Oxford gaoler. By the 1780s James and his brother Rev. Andrew Etty (1717–1784) had inherited valuable leases in respect of the castle. These had devolved to another member of the family, Charles Etty, by the time of the sale of the whole site by Christ Church in 1785.

immediately adjacent, the Company's new "house and offices" had been completed, with the first meeting of the proprietors apparently being held there on 13 April 1796. The available records are not conclusive, however, and as subsequent payments relating to the materials and labour costs of the building were made to a William Hulcup until the middle of 1797, it would seem that Harris did not supervise the construction, although it was presumably his own design that was followed. Described in a modern architectural guide as a "fine, plain Georgian house of five bays and two and a half storeys", by the 1840s it had become the residence of the Company's Chairman, David Durrell, and his large family. It is now the entrance lodge to St Peter's College.

FIGURE 8 The Oxford Canal Company cartouche. Made of Coade stone, it demonstrates an almost unprecedented collaboration of Oxford "Town and Gown", and may well have been designed by the gaoler Daniel Harris. [*Photo: Mark Davies, 2003*]

HARRIS THE ARTIST AND ARCHITECT

The entrance to the Oxford Canal Company's building in New Inn Hall Lane was originally embellished with the cartouche of the company seal which now sits atop the portico of the subsequent headquarters, Canal House (also in the ownership of St Peter's College), on Bulwarks Lane. It is evidence of a commercial enterprise brimming with confidence: Britannia's shield bears the arms of both the city and the University, juxtaposed with a river barge, the Radcliffe Camera, and the University Church of St Mary-the-Virgin (see Figure 8). It is, quite literally, a sign of the times: a unique public proclamation of Oxford "town and gown" collaboration – between academia, religion, and trade – inspired by a mutual dependence on coal. Daniel Harris evidently had a hand in its production, since when the Canal Company paid the Lambeth-based Coade Company £43 12s in December 1797 it was in settlement of the bill which had been "sent to Mr. Harris for the model of the company's seal". This seems to imply that Harris may have created the design himself – being the most logical reason for his involvement – and certainly this would have been well within his capabilities, since his artistic skills were also of the highest order.

For four consecutive years, Harris provided the artwork for the highly prestigious Oxford University Almanac, printed at this time by William Jackson. The views were of Magdalen College in 1789; All Souls College in 1790; Oriel College in 1791; and Corpus Christi College in 1792. This association with the University may be the reason why Harris was commissioned to build a new warehouse for the Clarendon Press in 1797. Now part of Wadham College, it stands adjacent to the King's Arms on Parks Road. For whatever reason, it took until 1803, five years after completion, for Harris to be paid the balance of his bill – a very considerable £667 3s 3d. It would be understandable if he nurtured some resentment over this very long delay, which could perhaps explain in part his determination to pursue an ill-advised legal suit against the University's bankers some years later.

Harris' only other known artistic endeavours – apart from his illustrations for Edward King's *Vestiges of Oxford Castle* – are a view of the Carfax Conduit published in 1793 and a watercolour of Braziers House near Wallingford, which was exhibited at the Royal Academy in 1799. The current Gothic façade of the seventeenth-century building was designed by Harris, and constitutes a rare surviving example of his architectural accomplishments. Another, however, is his modification of the façade of Churchgate House in Bampton, which featured as the home of the Crawley family in the television series *Downton Abbey*. All these activities were accomplished while he was still the governor of the prison, and between at least 1790 and 1807 he also advised on repairs to numerous bridges throughout the county and some turnpike roads.

FIGURE 9 Extract from Richard Davis' map of Oxford, published in 1797, showing the completed new outer wall of the prison, two wings, and the new entrance gateway. Also of note are (broadly clockwise from far left): St Thomas' Church; the Castle Mill Stream (flowing north to south); the terminus of the Oxford Canal (including the warehouse built by Daniel Harris); Gloucester Green and the City Prison; George Lane; St Michael's Church (adjacent to the former Bocardo); Corn Market; New Inn Hall Lane; and St Peter-le-Bailey Church.

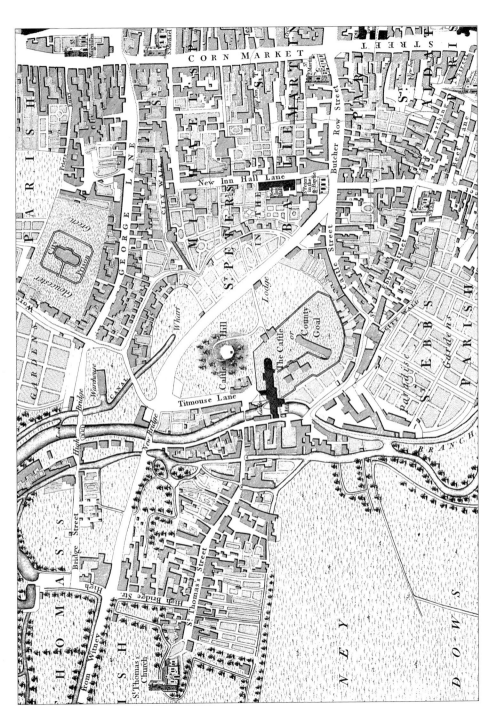

Daniel Harris' involvement with the Oxford Canal Company ended in 1801 in somewhat acrimonious circumstances. The commercial success of the canal had encouraged the Company to expand its Oxford operation by doubling the size of the original terminus and extending the canal itself closer to the city centre. Harris was engaged to undertake this work early in 1801, but a dispute subsequently arose in respect of the exact length of the extension that had been dug by the prisoners. It took nearly four years for the matter to be resolved, albeit 275 yards remained in dispute, the Company writing to Harris on 9 January 1805 to say, with some finality, that as far as they were concerned Harris had received all the payments due. Internal correspondence indicates the opinion that Harris was in severe breach of etiquette in making "an unusual and rude mode of application to the Committee" and behaving in an "indecorous" manner, and although the archival paper trail ends at this point, it is clear that Harris was not the most diplomatic of individuals, and the termination of the relationship seems likely to have left him with a certain lingering resentment.

Harris as Prison Governor (1787–1809)

Harris' enthusiasm for construction projects of all kinds was probably the salvation of many an Oxford prisoner. For although the practice of penal transportation to the colonies resumed at the end of 1787, Australia was still an unknown quantity, presenting far

FIGURE 10 St George's Tower by Daniel Harris in Edward King's *Vestiges of Oxford Castle* (1796). Work is only just beginning on the task of heightening the walls, suggesting that it was drawn some years earlier. The buildings in the background would seem to be in Tidmarsh Lane (called "Titmouse Lane" in Davis' map).

greater navigational challenges than America, and available vessels were scarce. Had Harris not contrived to involve himself in these local activities, where manual labour was in consistent demand, many prisoners would no doubt have found themselves suffering as many of their forerunners had, in conditions of overcrowding and soul-destroying inactivity. These labour-intensive projects provided every reason to keep prisoners in Oxford, however, where many went on to learn new skills while serving their sentences, to the great satisfaction of those who preached John Howard's philosophy of rehabilitation rather than retribution.

Howard's passion for his subject led him to visit many European prisons as well as English and Welsh ones, and he recorded his impressions in *An Account of the Principal Lazarettos of Europe etc.* (1789). He also took the opportunity to update his observations on some prisons closer to home. At Oxford his comments reflect well on Daniel Harris:

> Here the lodges, and the gateway with the chapel over it, will be built entirely by the convicts. These were at work, and guarded only by one man, though several of them, for their *good behaviour* had their irons taken off. This proves that amongst such delinquents many are reclaimable, and not so entirely abandoned as some are apt to suppose.

> Some prisoners, when they are discharged are completely clothed, have a little money in their pockets, and a good character given them, with a further promise that if they bring at the end of the year a certificate from the master with whom they work of a good and sober character, they will be further rewarded.

The bookseller Daniel Prince, whose house lay very close to the castle, was also full of praise in two 1789 letters (printed in John

Nichols' *Literary Anecdotes of the Eighteenth Century* in 1812). In July he observed that both new "magnificent" prisons (i.e. the city gaol in Gloucester Green too) were finished, that at the castle being in "a noble style, in imitation of the best old work". In September he wrote:

> The keeper, or governor as he is now styled, is an ingenious architect and mason, and contrives for the good of the publick, and the prisoners themselves, that a great part of the work shall be done by convicts, several of whom, by their industry and manifest reformation, have obtained their release at the expiration of two instead of three years.

Other means of reform were also being attempted. *Jackson's* of 21 April 1787 announced the magistrates' decision that

> in future persons bringing beer or victuals to any of the prisoners shall be obliged to deliver the same at the turnkey's lodge, and that no person, under any pretence whatever, shall be permitted to visit the felons upon Sundays.

It represented another success for John Howard, who had observed that in most other prisons Sunday was "a day of confusion and intoxication".

It was perhaps fortunate for Harris that in the 1790s Oxfordshire enjoyed a period of reasonable calm, possibly as a result of the relatively numerous employment opportunities to be found in the county. On 1 July 1792, for instance, *Jackson's* reported on a "maiden assize" (meaning one with no capital convictions) at which only two cases were heard. In January 1793 only three cases of felony were heard at the quarter sessions, and even those were for petty offences, prompting the newspaper to comment that "for some time past the gaol has been remarkably thin of prisoners, which must be chiefly attributed to the excellence of the county police, and the very active diligence of the magistrates". The compliment was repeated a year later, when the small number of prisoners was again noted at sessions in which only three people were tried (and all acquitted). On 3 May 1794, *Jackson's* reported a surely unprecedented occurrence, there being

> not a single prisoner now under confinement for any felony whatsoever. This affords additional proof, if any was required, of the very excellent police established in this county, which has been so frequently urged by the judges of assize as an example to other counties.

The term "police" does not mean an established force, it should be noted. Policing was still amateur and largely parish-based, but the Oxfordshire authorities did, it would seem, give greater support and encouragement to the individuals undertaking this role than elsewhere. Consequently, Oxfordshire was still leading the way in 1796: *Jackson's* commented on 9 April that the "the excellent police within the county" was the reason why only two prisoners had appeared at the assizes, and none at all at the quarter sessions, while in "every neighbouring county the prisoners for trial much exceeded the usual number".*

Continuous improvements and modifications were still being made to the prison buildings at this time, and some chance discoveries opened another avenue for Daniel Harris' multiple talents – archaeology. He would no doubt have had his appetite for the subject whetted by the discovery of a stone coffin in July 1789, recorded in *Jackson's* as being

---

* One could surmise that the small number of prisoners was, in part at least, due to a reduction in repeat offenders, owing to the new skills learned during Daniel Harris' tenure.

under the old wall of our castle nearly contiguous to the Great Tower, and within about 3 feet of the surface. In this coffin was a compleat human skeleton with this remarkable circumstance, that the skull was placed upon the bones of the feet.

The internal shape of the coffin, it was suggested, meant that "the head had been severed from the trunk before internment".* It was almost inevitable in the course of such major redevelopment of a site which had been occupied for so many centuries that unexpected subterranean discoveries would be made. (The same thing happened during the wholesale commercial redevelopment of the site in the 1990s.) Intrigued by some of Harris' discoveries, a historian called Edward King explored the site with him in 1794, and found the results so exciting that he felt compelled to expedite their publication. The result was *Vestiges of Oxford Castle* (1796), to which Harris contributed almost all the plans and illustrations (see Figures 3, 10, and 11).

King gave ample praise to Harris' contribution, noting that his "indefatigable labours … and skill as an architect and builder has enabled him to search out every part with minuteness". In so doing, Harris also delved into parts of the site which were not disturbed by the building work, and made new discoveries on the Castle Mound. Most notably, he investigated the vaulted chamber at the top, and discovered

in the floor of the room, a circular opening, four feet in diameter … walled up after the manner of a well, and filled with rough stone

---

* Harris would no doubt have been aware that when John Howard had visited Oxford in 1777, Solomon Wisdom had told him of the discovery of "a complete skeleton with light chains on the legs". Howard had surmised that these were probably the remains of "a malefactor who died in court of the distemper at the Black Assizes", a thought also aired by *Jackson's* at the time, in its issue of 21 March 1767 (see Chapter 5).

F. 2.

and rubbish, amongst which were found horses bones, dogs bones, and three or four horse shoes, and at a depth of about twenty feet, several human skeletons.

King also credited Harris with the discovery of the foundations of two three-foot-thick walls, evidence of the conjectured Norman hexagonal stone keep on the Mound, and also what King deemed to be "a curious little Saxon crypt". Harris had been obliged to modify its internal structure "in order to carry on the foundations of the great new buildings" – although only after recording the original arrangement with admirable precision (see Figure 11) – so that "each pillar stands about one foot and an half removed from its pristine situation".

The absence of retained county records often makes it difficult to know how many prisoners a gaoler might have been responsible for at any given time. James Neild included some helpful statistics in respect of the final years of Daniel Harris' tenure, however, in *State of the Prisons in England, Scotland, and Wales* (1812):

	Debtors	Felons
29 April 1800	17	37
23 Nov 1802	16	28
19 Aug 1803	14	15
30 Aug 1806	26	9
23 Nov 1809	5	19

FIGURE 11 The well room on top of the castle mound and the crypt "just as it appeared when first examined" near St George's Tower, drawn Daniel Harris for Edward King's *Vestiges of Oxford Castle* (1796).

Neild also described in some detail the function and size of each building, including:

The ground-floor of the old tower is the dungeon, 20 feet square and 20 feet high, ... used as a Black Hole, for the short confinement of those taken in an actual attempt to escape, or the very unruly and turbulent. The first floor contained a room of the same size as the dungeon below. It has a boarded floor, with one treble-bar iron-grated window, and is called 'The Condemned Hole'. The second and third stories [sic] contain each one room, of the same size as those below, but the keeper assured me that they had not been used these fifteen years. The upper room of this tower is of the same size as the others ... and is intended for the use of debtors (as formerly), if found necessary.

Neild also noted the continuing positive changes. The prisoners "are employed in sawing of stone or wood, or else in gardening, and have such a proportion of their earnings at the time of their discharge, as their good behaviour appears entitled to" and the site was arranged to allow "the keeper a convenient garden, which supplies not only his family, but the whole gaol, with sufficient vegetables".

HARRIS THE FAMILY MAN

It was in the church of her home parish of St Michael's that Susanna(h) Tomkins (c.1764–1822), daughter of a respected Oxford grocer, William Tomkins, married Daniel Harris on 4 June 1789. Apart from a stray reference to her as a child in 1775, when she happened to be travelling to Bath with her mother in the same coach as the New College diarist James Woodforde, she has eluded almost all historical mention. One must assume that she provided a self-effacing, domestic stability as a very necessary counterbalance to her husband's excessive busyness. And it is only an assumption, because Harris has left for posterity very few letters – and none, indeed, of a personal nature – and no journals, thus presenting inevitable difficulties in assessing his true character. His children – if they ever saw much of him – may have been equally unable to offer an opinion!

Apart from one short-lived son, all the couple's children were daughters. Harris outlived three of them, and also his wife, and although almost all of the funerals took place at the church of St Peter-le-Bailey, it was at St Thomas' that Daniel and Susanna had worshipped as a young couple. This is where their first three girls were baptised: Susan (1791–1835), Mary (1797–1889), and Martha (1799–1864). A fourth girl, Elizabeth (1801–1829) was the very first child to be baptised at a new chapel within the prison, on 3 April 1801. The baptism of a fifth daughter, Catherine, who was specified as Harris' youngest daughter when she died, aged 46, in 1850, has not been traced.

The Harris girls' lives were streaked with tragedy. In July 1827 Mary married John Barnard of Sawbridgeworth in Hertfordshire, but he died only a few months later, and she never remarried. Elizabeth married Thomas Dilly (1794?–1829) who in 1823 became governor of the prison, taking over from John Wyatt, who had succeeded Harris in 1809. She died "after a protracted illness" in June 1829, followed less than four months later by her husband, about whom *Jackson's Oxford Journal* commented: "the unfortunate prisoners under his care always found in him a humane master, ready to allow any reasonable indulgence their situation would admit of", prefaced by the assertion that "no prison in the kingdom has stood higher than Oxford for some years past in point of discipline". The other daughters – Susan, Martha, and Catherine – never married. Mary, whose married life in 1827 had lasted less than two months, returned to Oxford towards the end of her life, to live at what was called "Bulwark Cottage", New Road. She had retained her father's lease on a city property here, and the building in question – a clue is that it had a "subterraneous passage" under Bulwarks Alley – seems likely to be the former Conservative Club (very recently acquired by St Peter's College).

The Harris family grave is in Osney Cemetery, erected presumably after the demolition of St Peter-le-Bailey church in 1874. The names inscribed there are Daniel and his wife (as "Susan"), their daughters Elizabeth, Susan, and Mary, and Elizabeth's husband, Thomas Dilly. The stonework is, however, at the time of writing, in a dilapidated condition.

Harris also had a brother, Joshua (c.1767–1812), who from 1795 to 1797 was employed by the Oxfordshire magistrates as a weights and measures inspector, authorised to enter the premises or stalls of any persons "who shall sell by weight any wares, provisions, goods, or chattels" and to destroy any faulty equipment on the spot. Later Joshua worked for his older brother as the managing clerk of his building and architecture business.*

---

* *Jackson's* of 18 April 1812 noted his death in his 46th year. He was buried at All Saints on 14 April.

Harris the builder and architect
(1809–1840)

-+->-<-+-

Daniel Harris, it will be appreciated, was not your average prison governor. As such he was allowed considerable freedom by his employers, who knew a good thing when they had one, and they went to considerable lengths to retain his services. In 1808, his salary was nearly doubled to £200 "exclusive of an allowance of thirty pounds per annum for coals and candles". In addition Harris was to be paid £200, "out of the county stock as a remuneration for past services done in superintending the buildings of the castle gaol, and for an increase of his salary from the time of his first applying for the same". At the same Trinity sessions, however, Harris was given a mild reprimand in respect of his two turnkeys, whose weekly pay was raised to 15 shillings. This was presumably in acknowledgement of their additional responsibilities on account of Harris' frequent absences, since it was made clear that "it is the duty of the gaoler to give that situation his entire, regular and uninterrupted service". The comment shows that the multi-talented Harris was obviously prone to letting his attention wander from his responsibility for his staff. The pay rise was a final ploy to get him to concentrate on the basics of the job. It failed. Harris resigned the next year to pursue commercially what was evidently his real passion of architectural design.

A comprehensive list of Harris' architectural achievements can be found in Howard Colvin's *Biographical Dictionary of British Architects 1600–1840* (ed. 3, 1995), but three buildings are of especial interest: the new county bridewell at Abingdon (then in Berkshire); the novel installation of roofs made of paper in Eynsham; and St

Martin's Church at Carfax. He was still in charge at Oxford, in fact, when first publicly associated with the Abingdon gaol, designated as its surveyor in an advertisement for masons and builders placed in March 1806. There can surely have been no better-qualified architect for this job anywhere in the country than one who had spent 20 years as a prison governor! Five years later, the riverside building, using a modern three-wing radial layout designed to accommodate 32 prisoners, was complete, and the first keeper was appointed early in 1811 (see Figure 22). It closed in 1868, and has now (2018) been converted into private apartments.

Evidence of Harris' successful experimentation with the use of paper roofs appears in a publication on the subject entitled *An Account of the Paper Roofs used at Tew Lodge, Oxon.* Alluding to their ownership by the influential and long-established Eynsham family of Swann, the author J. C. Loudon stated (in 1811):

> The extensive mills, offices, and dwelling-house, at Ensham, have been covered with it by Mr. Harris of Oxford; a gentleman whose judgement in architecture and buildings is undoubted, and who ranks too high in his profession to sanction, by its practice, any uncommon material not preferable to those in common use.*

At about the same time, Harris found himself embroiled in a serious dispute with his bank. It appears to have been indicative more of his own stubbornness than of any genuine injustice that he took his case all the way to the King's Bench in London, and engaged the famous William Garrow (1760–1840) as his barrister. In an account of the verdict in *Jackson's* of 20 July 1811, his accusation of perjury by

---

* The flat-pitched roofs of the malthouse and cottages adjacent to the Swanns' former Eynsham home of The Gables are still evident.

Thomas Walker, Edward Lock, and Joseph Lock (partners in the Oxford University and City Bank) was dismissed. The case centred on the agreed repayment terms for a loan of more than £6,000 that Harris had taken out in June 1808.* The fact that Garrow, a man who "would never surrender while he could maintain a case", declared that "on this occasion he acknowledged that he ought not to trouble the defendants to go into further evidence" does rather speak for itself!

It also perhaps hints at Harris losing his grasp on reality. Certainly a few years later doubts were raised about his sanity, when negotiations were in train to sell the house and ground in New Inn Hall Lane which he had purchased from the Oxford Canal Company in 1797. The purchaser was the Methodist Church, and although it has been jocularly suggested that anyone at this time contemplating an arrangement with the Methodists might, *ipso facto*, find themselves to be considered mad, the situation was – briefly, at least – evidently a matter of genuine concern. Discussions for the sale began in June 1816, but in September the solicitor appointed to undertake the conveyancing, Charles Tomes, noted that it was Susanna Harris that he dealt with "owing to Mr. Harris's deranged state of mind". Tomes was merely listing his various meetings as part of his final reckoning, but his typical solicitor's zeal to account for every moment is helpfully revealing. In September, wrote Tomes, Susanna Harris was "ready to do any act in her power to carry the agreement in to effect". Her husband had rallied by the following month, however, Tomes being able to report on 31 October that "Mr. Harris was considered better".

---

* The fact that the bank was prepared to loan him such an enormous sum implies that his assets were sufficiently large by this time to justify the risk.

FIGURE 12 The signatures of Daniel and Susanna Harris on the conveyance of their New Inn Hall Lane property to the Methodist Church, dated 7 February 1817. [*With kind permission of the Wesley Memorial Methodist Church, Oxford*]

Not yet entirely so, though, evidently, since even a month after this his wife was only able to give the reassurance that "Mr H. was so much better as to afford a reasonable hope that he would be able in the course of 10 days or a fortnight to execute a general power of attorney authorizing a settlement of his affairs". His improvement continued, however, such that on 31 January 1817 Tomes was able to secure from a surgeon "his certificate as to the sanity of Mr. Harris". The conveyance was duly completed the following month, and the new Methodist chapel completed a year later (see Figure 12).*

Whatever the cause of Daniel Harris' mental breakdown, there appears to have been no reoccurrence, since within a couple of years he was engaged in perhaps his most ambitious ever building project: the demolition and rebuilding of St Martin's Church, in the very centre of Oxford, at Carfax, working in partnership with

---

* This episode is covered in *A History of Wesley Memorial Church, Oxford, 1818–1968* (1968) by J. E. Oxley. The chapel was later replaced by the current Wesleyan Memorial Church.

John Plowman. The first stone was laid in October 1820 and the first service held in the new building in June 1822.*

Daniel Harris died from "decay of nature" at his home in New Road on 13 June 1840, only minutes away from the prison to which he had contributed so much. His additional overall contribution to the success of the Oxford Canal and River Thames, and his concurrent and subsequent involvement in a range of architectural and building projects throughout the county, have earned him a richly deserved entire chapter in this book. His story has been in danger of being lost amidst the plethora of more famous names of which a city like Oxford can boast. Those names, however, are almost exclusively associated with the University, while apparently ill-educated men like Harris can all too easily sink unrecognised into the dunghill of history. In the insulting cartoon which marked his arrival in Oxford he was dubbed "damnable", yet he was, on the contrary, and in so many ways, damn able!†

Harris' resignation from the prison in 1809 marked the end of a momentous era in the history of Oxford Castle, and none of the other stories outlined in this book will stretch beyond that year. Having delved a little into the entire life of its most productive, if little-appreciated, governor, and some of his predecessors, it is time to consider some of the more exceptional men and women prisoners for whom they were responsible.‡

---

* The new building was demolished in its turn in 1896, leaving only the ancient Carfax Tower.

† A similar fate has befallen an Oxford contemporary of Daniel Harris called James Sadler (1753–1828), a pastry cook who became the first Englishman to fly, but whose lack of any association with the University has suppressed his fame (despite – again like Harris – additional achievements in many other fields). His extraordinary story is told in my biography, 'King of all Balloons'.

‡ The sole public acknowledgement of Harris is on the two lectern maps erected as part of the Oxford Canal Heritage Trail in 2014. See www.oxfordcanalheritage.org.

FIGURE 13 "The Old Tower from the Mill-stream" from James Ingram's 1837 *Memorials of Oxford*. The mill itself is hidden by the foliage of the tree. It is from this still extant tower that the Empress Matilda presumably made her escape in 1142.

CHAPTER THREE

ESCAPES AND "ENLARGEMENTS"

The resources available to the criminal-justice authorities of the eighteenth century were limited. Crime detection depended mainly on the abilities and enthusiasm of parish constables: individuals of varying degrees of ability and commitment, elected on an annual basis. More prominent figures such as a coroner, the keeper of the nearest prison, or even the local Justice of the Peace might become involved if the seriousness of the crime warranted it, but generally it was the individual parish that bore the brunt of the burden. Understandably, therefore, individuals with sufficient resources often took the law into their own hands, and there are plenty of examples of men with the necessary finances, influence, and time pursuing successful prosecutions through their own efforts.

Minor cases were decided at the local petty sessions, and more serious offences at the quarter sessions, held every three months or so, in the presence of local Justices of the Peace, who had a working knowledge of the law. More serious charges, usually including any for which a capital conviction was possible, were heard at the assizes, held in Oxford every March and July, before senior judges who made a regular circuit of the county towns of several contiguous counties. The venue for all the sessions was the Guildhall (on the site of the current Town Hall in St Aldate's), until a new County Hall (built by Daniel Harris' former business partner, John Plowman) was opened in New Road (on the site of the ancient Shire Hall) in 1841.* For the free-spirited individuals who typically found themselves behind bars, incarceration – even under reasonably civilised conditions – would have been a difficult thing to bear. As John Howard expressed it in his 1784 *Appendix to The State of the Prisons in England and Wales*:

> Convicts are generally stout, robust young men who have been accustomed to free diet, tolerable lodgings, and vigorous exercise. These are ironed, and thrust into close, offensive dungeons, some of them without straw or other bedding, in which they continue, in winter fifteen or sixteen hours out of twenty four, in utter inactivity, and immersed in the noxious effluvia of their own bodies.

Such conditions could be better tolerated if there was at least some sense of how long they would have to be endured – even if that did mean eventual transportation to an uncertain fate in the Americas. With the removal of even that prospect in 1775, however, with the outbreak of the American war of independence, it is perhaps unsurprising that an increasing number of men and women felt an additional compulsion to attempt to escape.

---

* G. V. Cox, in *Recollections of Oxford*, recalled the unsettling extremes to which the venue could be put in the 1790s: "I remember when the Town Hall, in which (in those hanging days) two or three poor creatures had been condemned in the morning to be hung for horse or sheep stealing, was hastily and tastefully *got up* for a County ball in the evening! – to be turned into a Court, at both ends, next morning!!"

The maxim "crime doesn't pay" is as selectively true today as it has always been, but for those men and women whose arrest or re-arrest warranted a reward, their endeavours did at least provide them with a kind of reward too: an immortality often denied those whose activities were far more notorious, or indeed meritorious. This lasting fame comes in the form of descriptions printed in *Jackson's Oxford Journal,* and occasionally the London press if warranted by the seriousness of the crime.* They do more than simply help modern readers to visualise the individual in question. Occasionally their age is mentioned, and a place of birth or domicile, providing helpful clues to identification, and students of fashion will find the clothing of interest. Also, because *Jackson's* often devoted considerable space to the method of escape, some interesting details about the extent and function of the castle buildings emerge. This chapter concentrates on some of the more ingenious, daring, or plain foolhardy escapes over a period of ten or so years until the rebuilding of the prison under Daniel Harris' supervision made escape almost, but not quite, impossible.

The Empress Matilda

-+>-<+-

For the most famous of all escapes from Oxford Castle, however, we need to go back to the twelfth century, even though it was not an escape made by a prisoner in the normal sense of the word. The Empress Matilda (or Maud) was the daughter of William the Conqueror's second son, Henry I, and although she was indeed a

---

* A high proportion of the criminal acts recorded in this book had some connection with London, either as the destination for stolen goods, or as the home of perpetrators of crimes on Oxfordshire soil, or as a place of refuge. It is for this reason that Sir John Fielding's increasingly efficient Bow Street Runners make occasional and telling contributions.

captive in the castle, she was there with many of her supporters, besieged by her cousin Stephen, who, like her, was a grandchild of William. In contesting the right to the throne, the two cousins brought England to a state of civil war. The situation came to a head in 1142, when Stephen's forces surrounded Oxford Castle, which Matilda had adopted as her headquarters because, as a contemporary chronicler observed (in what is known as *Gesta Stephani*), it was

> a city very securely protected, inaccessible because of the very deep water that washes it all round, most carefully encircled by the palisade of an outwork on one side, and on another finely and very strongly fortified by an impregnable castle and tower of great height.

The governor or constable at the time was Robert d'Oyley (nephew of the first custodian of the same name).* After three months, the situation had become critical. Matilda knew that she must surrender or flee. She chose the latter option, and, if her mode of escape one snowy December night is to be believed, she set a precedent for cunning which has never been equalled. There are several similar contemporary accounts of how she was able to cross the frozen River Thames undetected by Stephen's surrounding forces. Only one, however, that of Henry of Huntingdon, supplies the poignant detail that she and her companions were "clothed in white garments, which reflected and resembled the snow, deceiving the eye of the besiegers". Matilda made her way to the safety of Abingdon, then Wallingford, in an escape which had a fundamental impact on the subsequent history of Britain, and indeed Europe, since she was

---

* One of many Anglicised derivations of this Norman French name is Deeley. There is good evidence that families of this name in the Bicester area are descended from this second Robert d'Oyley, in which case so too is the current author: the ancestors of my great-grandmother Kate Elizabeth Deeley (1861–1925) were from Arncott, Launton, and Bicester.

able ultimately to ensure that her son would succeed to the crown as Henry II.*

Betty "Black Bess" Bing and her babes

-+->-<+-

Some six centuries after Matilda's epic escape, another woman of a rather different status made more than one attempt to follow suit. The story of the memorably named Betty Bing, alias Elizabeth Hughes, alias "Black Bess", demonstrates the dilemma of the authorities when dealing with mothers who had no means of support. The evidence is patchy, but within the bills that the gaoler (probably Marmaduke Etty) submitted over a period of six years a little of her intriguing story becomes apparent. It begins, however, in 1721, when she was being held at the Witney House of Correction on account of her "bastard child which is now living and is likely to become chargeable to the parish". In June 1726, according to the Calendar of Prisoners for Trinity 1726 (one of only a few to survive from this period), she had been apprehended near Chipping Norton in possession of a horse stolen in Shropshire. The bills submitted for her upkeep that quarter, under the name Elizabeth or Betty Bing, imply that she had absconded from the castle earlier that year, leaving a newly born baby behind, and possibly also the other older child. The bill for nursing one child covered 26 weeks to 12 July 1726, and another was for about three months' costs of "supporting Eliz. Bing and child in the time of

---

* Henry succeeded his uncle, Stephen, in 1154. Perhaps best known for his role in the murder of Thomas à Becket (after whom Oxford's St Thomas' Church is named), in the Oxford context Henry is most conspicuous for his adulterous affair with Rosamund Clifford, "Rosamund the Fair" (whose final resting place was Godstow Nunnery, described in *A Towpath Walk in Oxford*).

lying in" (or "groaning", as childbirth was also indecorously called). Evidently re-arrested, she was attended by a midwife at the assizes in July, and there was an additional cost for treating her child for measles. She was given the death penalty, but this was commuted to 14 years' transportation, although the sentence appears never to

"BENEFIT OF THE BELLY"

Bing's lengthy residence in the gaol raises the possibility that she invoked what was dubbed "benefit of the belly" (coined from "benefit of clergy", for which see Chapter 4). This dictated that a pregnant woman should be spared execution on the basis that the embryo was an innocent party. This loophole inevitably meant that if a condemned woman was not actually pregnant when arrested, she might well contrive to be so by the time of sentencing! One of the more salacious rumours about Oxfordshire's most notorious patricide, Mary Blandy, sentenced to hang in 1751 (see Chapter 6), was that she had been made pregnant by one of William Wisdom's sons.

The case of Mrs Mary Emerson, who was hanged in 1715, reveals that verification of pregnancy was not necessarily undertaken by a physician. Emerson (whom the Oxford diarist Thomas Hearne called a "notorious whore and thief" but also "a young woman, pretty handsome") had been found guilty of robbing a house in Garsington, and sentenced to hang. Within the Oxford Circuit documentation at the National Archives is the comment that she "pleaded her belly. A jury of matrons ... found her to be with child but not quick" (that is, dead in the womb). The sentence was therefore duly implemented.

have been carried out, leniency being exercised on account of either her existing child or her second pregnancy.

The considerable cost of providing food and clothes for "Betty Bing's child" was as regular a payment as any made by the county over the next few years. Yet she herself seems to have found the means to be self-supporting – there are no costs attributed directly to her – at least until early 1729, when the county again covered the expense of a midwife and nurse, along with "bread, cheese, ale, and fire" during her labour, plus "blankets, clouts, coats, shoes, stockings, frocks and food". In the bill for the next quarter, therefore, the charge was for two children and herself – although the baby girl died after only a few weeks.*

Her trial seems to have been delayed until after this, her second or possibly third pregnancy as a prisoner, was over, since a statement attached to the gaol delivery book for the March 1729 assizes confirms her conviction (as "Elizabeth Bing als Hughes als Black Bess") for the theft of two mares, though with what result is unknown. The county continued to support her surviving child for another four years or so, the last payment being logged early in 1733, when he or she must have been at least five years old. Over the years, Betty Bing alias "Black Bess" cost the county the very considerable sum of more than £60. In addition to her medical needs, these included, in the latter part of 1729, the additional costs of repairing two locks and to pay a mason for "four days work in building up the wall where the door was broke by Black Bess and her accomplices … endeavouring to make her escape". The gratitude of some people!

---

* St Thomas' burial register for 3 February 1729: "Elizabeth Binn, child of a prisoner in the castle".

A brothel keeper and a deer poacher

-+>-<+-

The proportion of *Jackson's* four pages that was devoted to local news rarely extended beyond a single column, and typically listed merely significant births, deaths, and marriages; political developments; and University appointments. Criminal acts often rated a mention, however, and escapes from prison almost always did. It can therefore be taken as a fairly reliable guide that no-one at all found the means to break out over the 20 years from the newspaper's launch in May 1753 until late 1774, when it carried the first such report.

The fugitive in question was Edward Clarke, 25, a former servant of Worcester College, who had been charged with keeping a disorderly house, in other words a brothel, in Friars Entry (near Gloucester Green). He escaped by scaling the wall of the castle on 13 September 1774. The offer of a reward was one of the most effective stratagems available to the hard-pressed and largely amateur enforcers of eighteenth-century justice, and Charles Wisdom, in one of his final acts as gaoler, offered five guineas for Clarke's capture. He was five feet tall, with a "smooth face, fresh complexion, picked nose, hazle eyes, and dark brown hair" and he was wearing "a fustian frock and waistcoat and leather breeches".

Two months later, a 40-year-old shoemaker called William Ward followed suit. This time it was the newly appointed Solomon Wisdom who provided the details, describing Ward as a former gentleman's servant from Charlbury who was "5 foot 6 inches high, fair complexion, light brown curled hair inclined to grey, ... sniffs with his nose often when he talks". He was wearing a "blue coat and waistcoat with yellow buttons, fustian breeches with a small stripe or rib, a small hat bound and partly cocked with hooks and eyes".

Finally, making one marvel that he got away at all, "he has a large rupture, which he endeavours to conceal by frequently holding his coat over the part".

Clarke was subsequently retaken, and made to stand in the pillory for an hour one Saturday in November, but what became of Ward is unknown. He seems previously to have suffered the same fate of being pilloried in his home town of Charlbury for stealing deer in 1768, and is presumably the same William Ward of Charlbury, described as a higgler (i.e. pedlar), who was convicted of the same offence in 1769 and of felling wood unlawfully in 1771.

Thomas Hilborne: a bigamist and a brawler

➤►◄◄

Escapes from Oxford Castle were all too often doomed to ultimate failure. In the case of an Oxford victualler called Thomas Hilborne, it was the escaper himself who was doomed, making his attempt in 1775 surely the least successful ever. Poor Hilborne had had an eventful year. He had been obliged to submit a personal apology, printed in *Jackson's* of 4 February 1775, for having assaulted William Prickett of Oxford, yet that same week was committed to the castle for another assault made in Magpie Lane.* At the March assizes Hilborne was sentenced to six months in the castle, both for this incident and for helping one Eleanor Jackson to escape from the city bridewell (at this time located on the castle site). Hilborne's own

---

* Lying just off the High Street, for centuries Magpie Lane had been a favourite haunt of prostitutes, and on this account had previously been known by an indecorously explicit Old English name. It was probably therefore the scene of as many disputes and affrays as anywhere in Oxford.

THE PILLORY

The pillory was a form of justice often favoured for its immediacy in cases where public ridicule was considered sufficient punishment – for instance, for dishonest tradesmen, slanderers, and (if they were fortunate) homosexuals. G. V. Cox in *Recollections of Oxford* viewed its effectiveness first hand in about 1794. Positioned near Carfax Church (probably in Cornmarket, near the Golden Cross Inn), "the poor wretch (with head and hands projecting through holes in the fabric) was now and then saluted with a rotten egg or some other worse missile. The pillory was a substantial structure, and high enough to expose the sufferer to the view of the jeering crowd." Because the victim/culprit was totally at the mercy of this mob justice, it was well worth taking a little trouble to win over a potentially hostile crowd. This was a line taken to good effect by William Blake in April 1765. Convicted like Edward Clarke of keeping a disorderly house (in St Giles'), Blake was brought up from the castle and put in the pillory at about 11 o'clock one Saturday morning. With a jocularity which perhaps reflected William Jackson's own opinion of the gravity of the offence, *Jackson's Oxford Journal* of 27 April 1765 described how, under the watchful eye of "a messenger of the Castle", Mr Blake "upon mounting the rostrum ... very judiciously bespoke the favour of the populace by a harangue to the following purport:- 'Gemmen, I hope nobody will millest me as I don't stand here neither for theft, nor murder, nor for suicide, nor sodomitical practices, nor yet for wronging no-body.' This pathetic oration had the desired effect, and Mr Blake not only stood unmolested, but, as it rained a little, was indulged by being covered with his hat during the great part of the ceremony." The Cornmarket pillory was last used in 1810.

botched escape was described in *Jackson's* of 10 June 1775. Described as a "resolute fellow", he had made several earlier attempts,

> having at one time nearly cut his way through the wall of the dungeon; at another almost forced a window frame on the north side of the prison; and at another perforated the wall of the room over the gate-way in order to fix a rope whereby he might scale the outer wall.

On this, his final attempt, he first placed a small bet with another prisoner as to the height of St George's Tower, in which they were being held in the uppermost room. Such wagers were probably commonplace as a means of injecting a modicum of interest into the tedium of incarceration, but Hilborne had an ulterior motive. In order to settle the bet, it was obviously necessary to measure the actual height, which he contrived to do by knotting together numerous small pieces of rope. When dangled from the window, this proved to be 15 feet less than the true height of 75 feet, but an accurate measure was not of course Hilborne's intention anyway, and he abseiled out of the window without delay. His makeshift ladder was unable to sustain his weight, however, and he plummeted to the ground. When help arrived he was still "quite sensible, but his limbs were so dreadfully fractured, and he had received so much internal injury, that he expired in about an hour". It later became apparent that his desperation to escape was driven by more than his fear of the sentence for his Oxford misdemeanours. He had also been charged with a capital felony in Somerset, and was a bigamist, and therefore had a rather greater incentive than many to try to avoid justice.

Elizabeth Boswell
and the unwise Wisdom

-+->-<-+-

The social status of these eighteenth-century escapees stands in some contrast to that twelfth-century pioneer of Oxford Castle escapes, the Empress Matilda. She remains as the most famous, but a woman of vastly different status should surely rate a close second, as the only person ever known to have escaped from the castle *twice*! For Elizabeth Boswell (alias Mason) was a humble Gypsy, born at Long Sutton, near Abingdon (i.e. Sutton Courtenay) in about 1756. Her story surfaces in May 1775, when she was arrested with her common-law husband, a tinker called James Corbett, for stealing goods from a shop in Beckley. Corbett was executed at Oxford on 14 August 1775, claiming, it was said, to be "happy in being prevented from committing further depredations upon the publick". Boswell, though expressing a desire to share the same fate, was instead given a sentence of 14 years' transportation. At the time this was still just about feasible, although delays and uncertainty were inevitable, as the ramifications of the American rebellion were assessed.

In the second edition of *The State of the Prisons in England and Wales*, John Howard observed that the women's night-room in 1780 measured only six and a half feet by four feet. For a woman accustomed to the freedom of a travelling Gypsy's outdoor life, confinement in a space little bigger than a coffin must have been especially hard for Boswell, especially as she succumbed to the dreaded contagion of smallpox and required nursing for the best part of a month. She had not long recovered when she made her first escape, in October 1776, by which time she had already been held for well over a year. With another woman, Rebecca Hall, she gained her liberty "through one of the windows adjoining the road, assisted, as it is supposed, by some of their accomplices, who cut out the iron bars, by the help of a ladder and drew them through the breach". The episode is made all the remarkable because Hall was "big with child" at the time, and it is indicative of the relatively small physical stature of people of the period that, although she was described as "stout made", she was able to squeeze her pregnant belly through a gap measuring only 17 inches by 12 inches.*

Solomon Wisdom duly issued descriptions of the two women. Ten guineas' reward was offered for Boswell, who was also "stout made" and about five feet seven inches tall, with "dark eyes, long brown hair, if not cut, fresh complexion, rather hangs her head down in her walk". Hall rated only five guineas and was five feet five or six inches tall, with "brown eyes, light brown hair, some of her teeth out before, on the upper part of her mouth, fair complexion".

Not surprisingly in view of the distinguishing impediment of her pregnancy, Hall was the first to be traced. She was returned to the castle and delivered of her child in December or January. Nursing during four weeks of "lying in" cost 36 shillings, with an additional 10s 6d each for the services of a manmidwife and apothecary, Anthony Rawlins, for two weeks, and a nurse for the same length of time. Further costs were lodged for maintaining her and her child for another 27 weeks, at 7 shillings a week, during which time she faced trial at the March 1777 assizes, but with what result is unknown: by the autumn, her name had vanished from the records.

---

* Hall had been born in Buscot, Berkshire in about 1755, and was in prison for stealing "two silver spoons, several pieces of bacon, wearing apparel and divers other goods" (*Jackson's* 29 June 1776).

Boswell's case was heard at the same March assizes. She had been recaptured at Tetsworth in February and conveyed to Oxford in a post-chaise, the owner of which duly received from Solomon Wisdom the reward of ten guineas. The statutory penalty for anyone who eluded custody before the period of transportation had ended (or even, in this case, begun) was death. Perhaps Boswell was sincere in wishing to follow her partner Corbett to the grave, because, on receiving a reprieve at this her second trial, rather than show contrition, she instead showed Solomon Wisdom a second clean pair of heels! She had to wait for almost another year, during which she again succumbed to an unspecified illness which required 15 weeks of nursing, but in February 1778 the opportunity to escape was contrived in this "most artful and long-premeditated" way, as *Jackson's* called it.

Boswell was alone in the "sick apartment", which was close to the condemned cell. This was "secured with two doors, the outer of which had a strong lock and two bolts, the inner two bolts". One of the condemned men, a highwayman called Robert Thacker, had sawn through the staple on both the lock on the sick apartment door and the one on the condemned cell's outer door, and then disguised his handiwork with cement. Boswell was therefore able to break out and release Thacker, who, with another highwayman, John Jones (alias Jefferson), then secured the doors again to avoid detection. Thacker then used his secreted saw to cut through their fetters, and together the three of them

forced their way through the side of the tower, upon a level with the high wall on the west side of the felons' yard, from thence by the help of the sheets from their beds, they let themselves down, over the iron spikes, into a garden adjoining the castle ditch, and got clear off.

Solomon Wisdom offered rewards of five guineas each for Thacker and Jones, but only two guineas on this occasion for Boswell, who was probably thought to have cost the county quite enough as it was! Her second escape was no doubt a huge embarrassment for Wisdom, who – as was shown in the previous chapter – did not exactly live up to the sagacity implied by his name!

> ## OXFORD CASTLE.
> **WHEREAS** on Sunday Night laft, the 1ft of February, 1778, the three following Prifoners found Means to make their Efcape, by breaking through the Wall of the Tower, viz.
>
> ROBERT THACKER, committed for a Highway Robbery, done near Maidenhead Thicket. He is about twenty-four Years of Age, 5 Feet 7 Inches high, by Trade a Taylor, was formerly a Bridewell-Boy at Black-Friers, with ftrait brown Hair; had, when he went away, a falfe Tail, wl ï'h might be tied on occafionally; hazle Eyes, hooked Nofe, thick Lips, high Check Bones, fmooth Face, ftrait made, and has a fore Leg.
>
> JOHN JONES, alias JEFFERSON, condemned March 5th, 1777, but reprieved. He is about twenty-four Years of Age, 5 Feet 2 or 3 Inches high; large grey Eyes, hooked Nofe, fwarthy Complexion, long Vifage, is ftrait made, fpeaks thick and fhort, with dark Hair, tied.
>
> ELIZABETH BOSWELL, alias MASON, aged about twenty-three Years, a tall and ftout-made Woman, born at Sutton, near Abingdon, Berks; frefh Complexion, light brown Hair parted before, hazle Eyes, a ftrolling Gypfey, under Sentence of Tranfportation.
>
> FIVE GUINEAS Reward for each of the Men, and TWO GUINEAS for the Woman, will be paid on their being delivered to the faid Goal, by me,
> SOLOMON WISDOM, Keeper.

FIGURE 14 The notice placed by Solomon Wisdom in three issues of *Jackson's Oxford Journal* in February 1778, following the escape of Robert Thacker, John Jones, and Elizabeth Boswell. Note that the capitals on nouns have generally been edited down in the text.

JOHN JONES
AND ROBERT THACKER

The exploits of **JOHN JONES** (24) had been described in some detail in *Jackson's* of 8 March 1777. He had stopped the Birmingham Fly (an express passenger coach) about three miles from Tetsworth on Milton Common. Most highwaymen had the sense to make themselves scarce once the deed was done, but Jones decided to chance his luck with a repeat performance on a coach called the Diligence later the same morning. It was not a smart move. Tetsworth was presumably already astir after one incident of daylight robbery, and the driver of the Diligence had no difficulty in persuading two armed men to return with him in pursuit. They got their man, but not without a struggle. Jones, "upon being called upon to surrender ... presented a pistol at one of the men, and threatened to blow his brains out, upon which without further ceremony the other fired his gun loaded with duck shot and dismounted the highwayman, wounding both him and his horse". Jones was found to have on him "a pair of pistols loaded with powder, a pair of bullet moulds, a spare flint, a crape hatband, a book of the roads with a leaf doubled down at the road upon which he then was, and 36 shillings in silver with some halfpence".

Within the subsequent quarter sessions documentation is a surgeon's bill for "attending John Jones, a felon who was wounded in the head and arms". The surgeon did what some might have considered an unnecessarily good job, because Jones was sufficiently recovered from his wounds one month later to make a first attempt to escape (along with the enigmatic Frenchman Peter le Maitre – see Chapter 4).

ROBERT THACKER, a tailor by trade, was described when he escaped as "about twenty-four years of age, 5 feet 7 inches high", with "strait brown hair, ... a false tail, which might be tied on occasionally; hazle eyes, hooked nose, thick lips, high cheek bones, smooth face, strait made, and has a sore leg".

Thacker had been imprisoned since October 1777, having been arrested for stopping a coach on the Maidenhead to Henley road. There had been eight people in the coach, but only two – Richard Taylor, landlord of the Bear Inn at Henley, who was deprived of his silver watch, and Bett Cox, who handed over half a guinea and a nutmeg grater – appear to have lost anything of value. At the time, *Jackson's* described Thacker and his accomplice Richard Latham as "notorious offenders", who had been active in London and elsewhere in the preceding three months.

Before Thacker's successful escape, he and Latham had attempted an earlier "enlargement", in December 1777. Four spring saws and a crowbar had been sent down from London by one or other's wife. These were "conveyed through a grate over the mill adjoining to the tower in which they were secured", but when an accomplice failed to appear, the tools were returned unused and taken to a local inn. There they were discovered "through the vigilance and uncommon assiduity of Sir John Fielding" (*Jackson's* 13 December 1777).*

---

* This appears to be the first reference in *Jackson's* to an involvement in an Oxfordshire case of Fielding's Bow Street Runners, two of whom later apprehended Thacker in London. Latham was executed at Reading in March 1778. It was Henry Fielding (1707–1754), the half-brother of John (1721–1780), who initially set up the fledgling force in 1749.

Expences occasioned by prisoners breaking Goal & escaping Feb.r j.t
in the night 1778

The Keeper with a Guard to London on Monday Feb.y 2.d in pursuit	£. s. d
of the [p]risoners paid the hire of two horses for 3 days	2 - 2 - 0
paid M.r Bond Sir John Fieldings Clerk to advertise in the London papers	1 - 1 - 0
expences on on the Journey	3 - 0 - 0
sending to several places different parties in pursuit ..	10 : 0 : 0
The Keeper with a Guard on Information of the prisoners lurking	
about Deddington & North Aston &.c two horses 3 day	1 : 10 : 0
paying the Guard & expences	2 : 2 : 0
paid the reward of bringing Elizabeth Boswell otherwise Mason to	
Goal Feb.y 26.th 1778	2 : 2 : 0
on Information of the prisoner Eliz: Boswell, that Jones and	
Thacker being at the Cross keys kept by a M.rs Kemp Harrow on the	
Hill paid the hire of post Chaise	7 - 0 - 0
paid a Guard with arms	0 : 5 : 0
Turnpikes and other expence	0 : 15 : 0
paid Simmons carriage to London & back	0 : 10 : 0
by who, oath the person of Thacker was Identified before	
Sir John Fielding	
paid Simmons for his time	0 : 10 : 0
paid M.r Jackson the printer for advertisements _ _ .	30 - 17 : 0
	1 - 16 - 0
Thackers account the reward _ _ _ _ _ _	5 - 5 - 0
Sir John Fieldings Men bringing the prisoner to Goal	3 - 2 - 6
paid their expences returning to London _ _ _	3 : 10 - 0
	44 17 - 6

Allow Mr Wisdom Fifteen Guineas
in part of the above Note tobe paid by the
County   Chris.r Willoughby Chairman.

Boswell, Jones, and Thacker initially stayed together, although Boswell remained at liberty for less than a month. *Jackson's* of Saturday 28 February 1778 reported her recapture, conveyed to the castle by a young gentleman who apprehended her near Wantage. The three fugitives had stayed at a public house in Faringdon the previous Tuesday and slept under a haystack near Wantage the following night. Boswell divulged that the two men had changed their clothes and hair styles – Thacker having tied his hair with a false tail, as mentioned in the wanted notice, while Jones had pinned his hair in curls (see Figure 14).

The two remaining fugitives found, as usual, that they had no place to hide. The bill submitted to the magistrates by Solomon Wisdom in relation to their arrests (see Figure 15) shows that searches were made in a number of locations, although in the end it was the men employed by the Bow Street magistrate Sir John Fielding who came up trumps. Once apprehended, Thacker was taken back to Oxford, from where he was transferred to Abingdon to stand trial (ultimately receiving the death penalty) in July 1778. The total bill for the capture of Boswell and Thacker came to the considerable sum of £44 17s 6d, including the cost of sending someone to London to make a positive identification. John Jones, whose capture was not included in Wisdom's bill, was ultimately, after a series of respites from a capital conviction, sentenced to "hard labour on the Thames". Elizabeth Boswell's third spell of incarceration lasted at least another year, as she was still present – and once more in need of nursing – in the summer of 1779. After that, however, her ultimate fate is unknown.

FIGURE 15 Solomon's Wisdom's bill for the pursuit of Jones, Thacker, and Boswell, and the arrest of the latter. The cost includes a guinea for "Sir John Fielding's clerk to advertise in the London papers". It was approved by Christopher Willoughby, chairman of the county magistrates. [*Copyright: Oxfordshire History Centre*]

Breaking out and breaking bones

->->-<-<-

The next year *Jackson's* reported the escape on 30 April 1780 of John Harper, a 20-year-old baker from Woodstock, accused of bestiality, and three deserters: William Helford, William Fawdry, and Richard Wells (33). Harper and Wells (whose own desertion was from the Oxfordshire militia) had been confined within St George's Tower, and

> having found means to break their way through the wall above the door-case in the side of a chimney almost adjoining, got upon the stair case and forced the lock of the Little Dungeon, where the two other deserters were confined. Having done this they likewise forced off a large iron bar which went quite across another door upon the tower stair case, which serving as an iron crow, enabled them to force that door and likewise break through the staircase wall of the tower, about 30 feet from the ground, from whence they let themselves down with ropes.

Harper and Wells "were seen the same day at Bruckin's Weir near Ensham, and again at Cote, near Bampton, where a farmer hid them under some straw". The farmer's motive is unclear, but both men could easily have been known to him, as Harper was born in Eynsham and Wells was from Bampton, where he worked as a collar maker. Harper later acknowledged a classic near-miss at this point, in revealing that "the hangar with which the straw was probed, in one of the thrusts, grazed against his cheek".* Wells continued into Wiltshire and helped himself to a horse there on

---

* A hangar is an iron hook used for suspending items above ground.

9 May, before returning to his home village of Bampton, where his wife and family lived. Word evidently leaked out, however, as a party of marines was sent to the village in disguise soon after, and lured Wells into falling for one of the oldest tricks in the book. According to a broadside (a printed account of his life and execution, of a kind offered for sale at many public hangings), one of the disguised marines "entered the house where he had secreted himself, and affecting great friendship informed him that there were several people in the town in quest of him, advising him at the same time to make his escape by the back door". There, needless to say, several marines were lying in wait, and Wells found himself escorted swiftly back to Oxford Castle.

Wells was found guilty of horse-theft at the following assizes, and executed on 30 August 1780. He was said to have been wayward from youth, and a bad father and husband – yet his wife attended him affectionately in prison, and he is quoted as expressing regret "that his wife and children would be *twitted* with his misfortune".* On the fatal day, according to *Jackson's*, Wells

> seemed rather in a hurry to get rid of the world. For after the cord was fixed, he almost instantly gave a signal for the executioner to turn him off, and not finding the man so quick as he expected, called to him to know what he could be about, adding *for God's sake turn me off.*

He had been a bell-ringer in Bampton, and asked that when "his corpse arrived there, the bells might be muffled, and that his

---

* Wells was baptised at Bampton on 24 October 1746, and married Rose Stone on 26 August 1777. The very next day, Rose, under the name Wells, was back in church to baptise her daughter, Elizabeth. The couple had another daughter, Rose, baptised on 27 March 1779. The quarter sessions documentation shows that Richard had been found guilty of several assaults in 1771, 1772, and 1775.

companions might honour his memory with a dumb peal". What became of Harper is unknown.

A similar escape was reported in *Jackson's* of 15 September 1781. Unfortunately for James Eldridge, a deserter, Richard Geden (of St Thomas' parish), and Nicholas Hemmings, it was also reported by a large number of people who saw it happen! It was 7pm and still light when the three men broke out "by forcing the door of the felons' hall, and breaking through the tower stair case about 10 feet above the ground from whence they let themselves down by tying together the sheets from their beds". Only Eldridge avoided recapture, the unfortunate Geden having broken his leg in the attempt.*

"A very artful defence": Joseph Simmonds and his gang

➤➤◄◄

It is intriguing to learn from the preceding stories that the clichéd image of prisoners escaping from castle towers by shinning down ropes or makeshift ladders made of sheets has some basis in fact. But prisoners found other uses for sheets too: Thomas Haddon used his to effect an "escape" of a more permanent and drastic nature. Haddon (presumably the same who was baptised in Charlbury on 24 February 1763) had been arrested for robbing the Banbury Mail outside the King's Arms at Deddington in February 1782.

---

* *Jackson's* had identified Geden as the apparent victim of an assault "with the intent to commit an unnatural crime" by one Richard Tarrant earlier that year. Tarrant was sentenced to two years' imprisonment in the castle, to be whipped, and also to pay immediately the astonishingly large sum of £50 (*Jackson's* 2 June 1781). But Geden himself was then brought in the following month charged with committing "a most odious crime" with Tarrant the previous January. He too received the same sentence of two years in prison for "sodomitical practices" and "during that time to be thrice severely whipped" (*Jackson's* 28 July 1781).

His accomplice, William Holmden, was a marine who had come to Oxford as part of a recruiting party. Haddon was arrested at Warwick and duly condemned to death at the Oxford assizes of July 1782, Holmden having "admitted King's evidence" (i.e. turned informer) after being apprehended in Portsmouth. But before the sentence could be carried out, *Jackson's* informed its readers, Haddon found the means to hang himself from an iron bar in the window of the condemned cell "by tearing the sheets of his bed and fastening them to his garters". As was common practice with suicides, his body was interred in the public highway, in this case the Botley Turnpike Road, "without coffin, tho' he had provided one previously". As will be seen in subsequent chapters, corpses were in much demand in Oxford for medical lectures, and it is indicative of the superstitious dread with which anatomisation was held that Haddon's friends, "as soon as the body was thrown into the grave, ripped open his belly, and filled it up with unslaked lime, to prevent its being taken up for dissection". The body of an executed highwayman Isaac Darkin (see Chapter 6) had been subjected to the same drastic attention in 1761.

Haddon was part of a large network of Oxfordshire criminals. Two others who were brought in on Holmden's evidence were Joseph Simmonds, keeper of some livery stables in George Lane, and his employee Paul Ragg. After the robbery at Deddington, Haddon and Holmden had ridden to Oxford, where Simmonds and Ragg helped to burn the incriminating evidence of the mail bag and its unwanted contents. The authorities were quickly in pursuit, and although Haddon and Holmden had already left the premises, Simmonds was discovered asleep in bed. Joseph Simmonds was a resourceful character, however, as the tale of his next few years will show. He roused himself sufficiently to escape barefoot across

Gloucester Green and hid in a house opposite Worcester College "by getting a considerable way up the chimney, and from whence he refused to come down till he was threatened to be fired on". A subsequent search of Simmonds' house in George Lane revealed a large cock and hen which had been stolen the previous night from the Catherine Wheel at Sandford. Now alerted to more than just the Banbury Mail robbery, the authorities expanded the search. At his farmstead in Wallingford, Simmonds' brother, Robert, was found to have two stolen copper tanks and 30 sheep skins, the latter taken from a garden near the castle. And on Haddon's evidence, three horses stolen from Herefordshire were recovered, one of them from Simmonds' father, John, also in Wallingford.

In June 1782, the Simmonds brothers and Ragg were joined at Oxford Castle by two more of the gang named by Holmden. These were two Oxford labourers, James Slatford and William Best, who were summoned to explain their part in the burglary of the house of Mrs Fredericks of Bampton in the previous January. The five men had been interrupted when a servant girl managed to slip out and raise the alarm, causing them to make a hurried departure. The extraordinary reward of £50 immediately offered by Mrs Fredericks for the apprehension of the thieves was matched by the residents of Bampton, reflecting a general desperation among rural communities concerning conventional methods of detection.

Despite the discovery of a distinctive piece of evidence, Best's hat, the Fredericks burglary was not proven against any of them at the March 1783 assizes. However, Slatford (then 36), Best (33), Ragg (38), and Joseph Simmonds (29) *were* found guilty of burgling a house near Christ Church more than a year previously. For this, all four were given sentences of seven years' transportation to Africa (the west coast being a destination to which, it was hoped, a small number of transports could still be sent during this interim period between the last ships bound for America and the first destined for Australia). That there is no further mention of Robert Simmonds (32) rather suggests that he, like Holmden and Haddon, might have turned informant.*

Joseph Simmonds was not a man to sit on his heels, however, and on 17 July 1783 he attempted to improve on his earlier unsuccessful foray not-quite-far-enough up that nearby chimney. The announcement of his escape gives us a visual image of the former mercer's apprentice, as five feet six inches tall with "hazle eyes, thin smooth pale face, brown curling hair, a small mole on his left cheek" and "several boils, particularly one under his chin". William Best accompanied Simmonds in his flight over the wall of the debtors' yard. He was described as a timber sawyer of 33, five feet seven inches tall, and born in Oxford.† He had "grey eyes, but has lost the sight of the right eye, brown straight hair, thin face, pale complexion". Both men were deemed by Solomon Wisdom to have a "sallow countenance from sickness".

Best was recaptured at Botley within a couple of weeks. At the next assizes, in March 1784, his sentence of seven years' transportation was changed to death on account of "being found at large in this kingdom without any lawful cause before the expiration of the term for which he was ordered to be transported to Africa". This was a common charge levelled at apprehended escapees, often preferred to any additional charge of actual escape from custody. Nonetheless,

---

* It is quite likely that Robert Simmonds was the unnamed brother involved in Joseph's later re-capture in London, with its hint of a set-up. The parish records of St Mary's in Wallingford reveal that Robert was baptised on 5 June 1751 and Joseph on 16 April 1753, showing that caution is needed with the stated ages in the Calendar of Prisoners, where Robert was noted as being 27.
† Most likely the son of William & Mary Best baptised at St Ebbe's on 29 March 1751.

the death penalty was only rarely invoked for physically able young men guilty of unaggravated theft, and Best's sentence was commuted to transportation for life.

Best may have failed to enjoy his liberty for long, but Simmonds was made of sterner stuff, and it was not until October 1783 that he was traced. Even then, it took an elaborate scheme to trap this wily character, involving the collaboration of the Oxford and London authorities. Thus it was that John Smith (the keeper of the Oxford City Gaol) and a constable, Richard Spindlove, succeeded in luring Simmonds and his brother (unnamed, but probably Robert) to join them for supper at a Westminster hostelry. During the meal, four officers from Bow Street pounced, among them Mr Jealous and Mr Clarke (who feature in at least one other successful arrest on behalf of the Oxfordshire authorities), and Simmonds was taken back to Oxford. This time he was held in the lower dungeon "from whence", *Jackson's* reported with satisfaction on 25 October 1783, "it may be presumed, no small difficulty will attend any future attempts for an enlargement". The newspaper was only partially correct.

Simmonds' spirit cannot be doubted, whatever his other short-comings; nor can his popularity among his peers, who connived in at least two more of his attempts to avoid justice. On 20 December 1783, *Jackson's* reported the discovery that Simmonds' fetters had been weakened by using a tool made by "forming about three inches of that part of a case knife next the handle into a kind of chisel, probably carried thither in the mouth [sic] of some of the prisoners." Pewter had been smoothed over the severed chain, in anticipation of breaking out after an inspection, but the ploy was detected.

Simmonds' final attempt, a desperate last throw of the dice only days before his hearing (at the Easter quarter sessions, for some reason, rather than the March assizes), was reported in *Jackson's* of 17 April 1784. Again, outside help was apparent, as Simmonds' wife had

> found means to convey into our castle a couple of back files, in a clean shirt, sent to one [Thomas] Owen, a locksmith, one of the capital convicts reprieved at our late assizes, and being also possessed of two strong clasp knives, for saws, the felons found means to cut away the thin bars placed before the dungeon window to prevent any attempt upon the strong ones behind. Having thus far succeeded, and Simmonds having administered an oath of secrecy (upon his prayer-book) to each of his companions, the night following was to have covered their enlargement. But on Thursday morning, upon their being unlocked at the usual hour, William Furnell alias Cherry, another reprieved convict, gave information to the keeper, who seized the implements, and it has since been found requisite to chain these most daring as well as turbulent offenders, by night, to the floor of the dungeon in which they are confined.

Simmonds received the death penalty a few days later. Technically, as for William Best, this was "for having been found at large in this kingdom before the expiration of the term for which he had been sentenced to be transported". The spirited Simmonds made what *Jackson's* called "a very artful defence", however, and his sentence, again like Best's, was commuted to life banishment. It was another eight months or so before he took his final departure, given the lack of transportation ships at this time, and he was taken first to Woolwich to be held on a hulk called *Censor* (*Jackson's* 8 January 1785).* Three other prisoners accompanied Simmonds on his travels.

---

* By April 1784, Joseph Simmonds' comrades had all already been removed (William Best for life, Paul Ragg and James Slatford both for seven years) for onward passage to Africa. They were among a total of 22 convicts dispatched from the castle in March (see Chapter 4).

Two of them were John Hawkins and William "Bumper" Smith, both from Oxford, the latter being the only man noted as having successfully escaped from the castle only to turn himself in again.

A gang of Oxford burglars

-+>-<+-

William Smith and John Hawkins were ordered to be transported for a burglary committed exactly a year earlier. The details were recounted in *Jackson's* of 31 January 1784. The break-in had occurred at the premises of an Oxford grocer, Isaac Lawrence, who had lost £37, some earrings, some port, and some cheese. Hawkins and his brother Richard were known offenders, and suspicions were raised when they were observed to be spending freely on the same evening at a public house in George Lane, in the company of Smith, another Oxford labourer called Edward Ladds, and "some girls of the town". When the Hawkins' lodgings in St Thomas' parish were searched the next day, some of the money was found, and John Hawkins was seen to pass his brother a small box which "he found means to throw into the river". It was recovered, however, and found to be Lawrence's snuff box. Meanwhile, Smith and Ladds had sniffed danger and tried to flee, but got only as far as Medley House, on the Berkshire side of the Thames near Binsey.* Ladds immediately confessed, saying his role had merely been to stand watch while John Hawkins and Smith entered the premises.

Ladds was shown leniency for his candour and minor role, and Richard Hawkins' involvement had been merely incidental, so only

---

* At this time Medley Manor was owned by my four-times great-grandfather, Cork-born Matthew Leslie, who spent his whole adult life in India. For more about this strange coincidence, and about Medley as a destination for pleasure parties, see the *Oxford Times' Limited Edition* magazine of November 2016 and *A Towpath Walk in Oxford*.

John Hawkins and William Smith faced trial at the quarter sessions in April. Their initial death penalties were subsequently commuted to transportation to America for life for Hawkins (Nova Scotia being thought – optimistically – as a feasible destination after the Treaty of Paris of 3 September 1783), and 14 years in Africa for Smith. When the latter escaped, an unusual double reward was offered in a notice in *Jackson's* of 17 July 1784. Solomon Wisdom offered the customary five guineas for information leading to his arrest, or ten guineas for anyone who actually apprehended him, and an identical sum was offered in addition by the Oxford Corporation. Smith, who had been born in St Peter-le-Bailey parish, very close to the castle, was described as being five feet nine or ten inches tall, and aged about 22, with "dark grey eyes, strait dark hair, fresh complexion, stout made … has sores upon both his legs, and had on a blue coat, green and white waistcoat, and long trowsers".* The notice was unnecessary, and the rewards unclaimed. Within a fortnight of his escape, as *Jackson's* related on 24 July 1784, Smith "surrendered himself by knocking at the castle gate and requesting to be re-admitted to his old apartments". What happened to him next is unknown.

James Hanks: convict and (Australian) gentleman

→>‹←

It is difficult to assess the preceding incidents, observed briefly and imperfectly more than two centuries after the fact. The very regular succession of escapes and attempted escapes during Solomon

---

* Probably William, son of William and Elizabeth Smith, baptised at St Peter-le-Bailey 10 December 1760.

Wisdom's tenure as governor was probably as much to do with the sudden overcrowding caused by the cessation of transportation to the American colonies and the simultaneous dilapidation of the buildings as it was to Wisdom's lack of diligence. The true motives and natures of the fugitives, meanwhile, can only be surmised. Admiration, sympathy, and distaste are aroused in approximately equal measure. However, it should be noted that every one of these "enlargements" occurred before the major building works of the 1780s. So the first escape to have occurred after the construction of the new, sturdy outer curtain wall and new cell blocks makes its perpetrator all the more remarkable. James Hanks, from Hanborough, was obviously among the most determined and athletic of those individuals who successfully eluded the confines of the castle. Sadly for his chances of being able to indulge in leisurely enjoyment of his triumph, however, he was also among the most imprudent!

Hanks had been arrested in August 1793 for "burglariously entering the lodgings" of Rev. Friend, the Principal of New Inn Hall, from whom he took cloth, gold, and silver. He was also accused of stealing a watch from the house of Samuel Denton of All Saints. Hanks was inconvenienced for only a matter of days. Within a week of his arrest, he contrived an escape "from the felons building … by breaking through the grating that encloses the day room", and from there scaled "the boundary wall towards the Castle Mills, and got from thence through an adjoining garden". A notice placed in the next issue of *Jackson's* offered a reward of ten guineas above the statutory sum. Hanks (22) was described as five feet five and a half inches tall (the specification of the half being, perhaps, indicative of Daniel Harris' fastidious attention to detail!), "well made, fresh complexion, hazle eyes, brown hair" and was wearing "a light coloured coat, striped waistcoat, buckskin breeches, worsted stockings, and a round hat", giving him the "appearance of a groom".

In a second otherwise identical notice a week later, an additional reward of five guineas was offered by John Smith, keeper of the city gaol, who was at pains to point out that it was he who had apprehended Hanks initially, but that the prisoner had been the responsibility of the county authorities at the time of his escape. Smith's comment might be read to imply carelessness on the part of Harris, but, on the contrary, he managed to emerge from even this embarrassment with credit. In making a payment to him of £19 5s 6d "for apprehending and retaking" Hanks, the magistrates commented that the "escape was not effected through any negligence of the said Daniel Harris, but on the contrary that the said Mr. Harris had taken every precaution".

It had taken Harris less than a month to retrieve his man. In some respects, it is surprising that it took so long, because Hanks had made scant effort to cover his tracks. He had swiftly found employment at Woodstock, and had the nerve to show his face in Oxford on several occasions. Indeed, on the day of his re-arrest, he had taken an early coach into Oxford, where he had taken breakfast at the Cross Inn (that is the Golden Cross, off Cornmarket), and then got the Worcester coach back to Woodstock. But someone there had finally recognised him. Even then, Hanks' admirable bravado very nearly carried him through, when "he called himself Smith, and so boldly confronted those who challenged his person that for a while they became rather doubtful of his identity", as *Jackson's* put it on 16 September 1793. Only the arrival of the city gaoler John Smith, a man who really could identify him, settled the matter. Hanks was ordered for removal to Botany Bay in Australia in the following May, although it took several years before he actually departed, travelling on the *Barwell,* which sailed from Portsmouth on 7 November 1797.

It is easy to warm to a resourceful, audacious, but seemingly ingenuous character like Hanks, who, as it transpired, adapted well to the untried opportunities of a new life under Australian skies. Once he had served his sentence he became, with a certain poetic justice, a member of the Sydney Loyal Association, essentially the local police force, and raised a family with another transported convict, Sarah Trapnell of Bristol. By the time of his death in 1843, Hanks had acquired property and status, being described as a yeoman in his will and as a gentleman on the death certificate.*

James Hanks, then, made a success of his banishment. He was by no means alone in that. We may never know the ultimate fates of hundreds of others whose stay in Oxford Castle was a prelude to a long trip on a transportation vessel, and a rather longer stint of hard labour at the end of the voyage. But we do know some of the reasons why people found themselves in this predicament in the first place, and the following chapter outlines but a few of the more interesting examples.

---

* See *James Hanks, Convict & Gentleman*, a self-published 1993 typescript by Keith W. Hodgson (at the Oxfordshire History Centre), and *Convicts & Currencies* (2006?) by Anthony Laffan, neither of which, however, mentions Hanks' intrepid few weeks of hard-won liberty.

CHAPTER FOUR

HARD LABOUR:
"AT HOME" AND ABROAD

The first ships to transport criminals to America reached Georgia in 1607, but it was not until 1718 that an act was passed which standardised the practice, making it more viable for shipowners to undertake the task. With few exceptions, from then on criminals found guilty of serious non-capital offences were sentenced to seven years' hard labour overseas and those reprieved from capital convictions were condemned to 14 years. Anyone detected on British soil before the expiration of their sentence (either by escaping before the sentence had begun or by managing to find a passage back home) received a new life sentence. Given the very large number of offences for which the death penalty could be allocated – more than 200 by the beginning of the nineteenth century – this produced a very regular supply of candidates, as judges tended to avoid actual executions whenever possible. However, soon after the first stirrings of revolt against British rule in America in April 1775, preferred destinations such as Maryland, Virginia, and Georgia became inaccessible. For a few years Nova Scotia and West Africa were considered as replacements, but generally for those men and women who would otherwise have faced a period of forced labour overseas their destination proved no more exotic than a Thames' hulk at Woolwich. The first transportation ship to Australia sailed in May 1787, but it was several years before this distant and untried destination could confidently accept the large numbers of miscreants of which the "Old Country" was still so very keen to be rid.

Transportation: "partes beyond the seas"

→►◄←

The names of the earliest known Oxfordshire residents ordered for transportation appear in an order signed in Whitehall on 13 July 1617. Whether these five "prisoners in Oxford Goale" – Christopher Potley, Roger Powell, Sapcot Molineux, Thomas Middleton, and Thomas Crouchley – actually reached the intended destination of Virginia is unknown. The order was in any case not entirely prescriptive, understandably in view of the logistical difficulties involved, and the deliberately flexible alternative of "other partes beyond the seas" was added.

The surviving Oxfordshire quarter sessions records begin in 1687, and in the Calendar of Prisoners for 5 April 1687 William White of Benson is noted as facing the sentence of transportation. It was some time before the necessary arrangements could be made, however, by which time four others had been similarly sentenced: John Carter, a miller from Shipton (for burglary), a second William White (for horse-theft), Thomas Webster (for horse theft), and Peter Beer (for stealing a basket of linen). All but the latter were ordered to be removed on 15 August 1688, the gaoler (presumably Elizabeth Thorpe) being required to deliver them to the keeper of

Gloucester Gaol, "who hath undertaken to transport them". All four had been removed from the castle by May 1689. Beer had apparently been reprieved.

This is the pattern of evidence on which this chapter is based: a record of the sentence in the Calendars of Prisoners, the issue of an official order to transport from the under-sheriff, the bill submitted by the gaoler for conveyance to the ship, and the subsequent absence of the prisoner's name in the castle records. It is evidence which is not conclusive. The documentation is incomplete, and it should be noted that, simply because an official order was made for a person's transportation, it does not necessarily follow that he or she actually made the journey, nor survived the voyage, or even lived long enough to embark on it.* Each case of transportation needed the authorisation of the Secretary of State before the Oxfordshire under-sheriff could prepare his orders. There might then be a further delay while a suitable ship was located. In the interim, it is possible that some prisoners might have escaped, or died, or been reprieved before physical relocation was achieved.

It appears that no further instances of transportation from Oxford occurred until late 1694, when three horse-thieves, John Jeffreys and Robert Smyth (both of Nettlebed), and James Platt were removed, assuming, that is, that their request to enlist in the army as an alternative failed. Henry James of Bampton (for highway robbery), and the first known Oxfordshire female transport, Elizabeth Norton of Deddington, who did definitely sail for America, followed in 1695.

The next two references are, unusually, to individuals who had

---

* Interested readers should consult Peter Wilson Coldham's alphabetical *Complete Book of Emigrants in Bondage* (1988) and his subsequent publications on the topic (see Sources).

already been removed. A comment on the prisoners' bread bill for Michaelmas 1700 stated that Edward Franklin (of Bullingdon Green) and John Woolhams had been transported on 7 September 1700. Franklin, of Horspath, had been found guilty of stealing oats from Edward Ford of Garsington, a crime deemed worthy of banishment to the colonies on account of his other thefts of three years earlier: of bees, hoes, and a ladder.

At Easter that same year of 1700, Mr Etty (presumably Andrew) had been instructed to remind the justices at the next session to pay the Gloucester gaoler for costs incurred in the transportation of old John Staite. It is worthy of comment that Staite (also styled Stayte and Steat) was defined as "old". There was a logical tendency to show leniency to older men, especially those with families. The motive was not necessarily compassionate: if a transported man left behind him a young family, they were likely to become a burden on their parish. And of course the colonies preferred younger individuals, able to contribute their full quota of physical effort. Staite, however, was a habitual offender, having already experienced confinement in the castle in 1690 for clipping coins (see Chapter 5) and in 1696 for burglary. His third offence, taking £16-worth of gold and silver from the house of Elizabeth Dobson of Aston Rowant in 1698, earned him the death penalty, commuted, old or not, to transportation.

Staite was the last Oxfordshire transport verifiably to leave via Gloucester, probably for onward delivery to Bristol (although it appears that he may have died before or during the voyage). In the 1720s, transports from Oxford were taken to Bristol direct. In the quarter sessions documentation for Epiphany 1723 there is a bond for £200 issued on 7 December 1722 to a Bristol merchant called Jonathan Becher (and witnessed by Marmaduke Etty). Of the eleven prisoners named, four were not actually from Oxfordshire, although they had committed their felonies in the county. Six people had been found guilty of grand larceny, and, on account of the 1718 Transportation Act, faced specific sentences of seven years. These were Thomas Lowe (a butcher of Bampton), Sarah Cooke (spinster of Burford), Thomas Pickmore (a labourer of Oxford), Richard Waine (a stonecutter of Milton), and John Trentham and Benjamin Burrell (both butchers of Deddington). The eleventh prisoner, Richard Cooper, an Oxford labourer sentenced to 14 years for burglary, had pleaded "benefit of clergy" – a late instance of this centuries-old means by which influential members of society eluded the justice meted out to the less educated.* The contract stated that Becher must acquire a certificate of delivery from the governor or chief customs officer of the destination colony within four months of the date of the bond, and present it to the Oxford Clerk of the Peace within a year to receive payment. It appears to be the only example of such a contract retained in the Oxfordshire records, but all other instances presumably contained similar stipulations. Because payment was made only after delivery, and per individual, it encouraged the merchant to take good care of his human cargo, which Becher did, apparently, in this case, since all those named did (according to Coldham) all arrive on American soil.

Further orders for transportation occurred erratically until about 1730, with groups of convicts conveyed every few years, seemingly

---

* "Benefit of clergy" had originated as a means by which miscreant churchmen could have their cases heard at an ecclesiastical court, rather than at a more stringent lay court, simply by proving that they could read the opening verse of the 51st Psalm. The term stuck when its scope was widened to enable courts to apply leniency to anyone who could read. The practice was officially abandoned in 1706, although the phrase (and test) continued to be used as a means of avoiding the common punishment of branding on the hand for petty thefts until 1827.

always via London from 1724 onwards. From 1737 until 1775, when the practice ceased, the removals were on a near-annual basis. Almost without exception the crime was theft – very often of the most trivial nature. James Norford was transported for stealing some handkerchiefs in 1746, for instance, and Richard Dyer for stealing peas in 1758. But perhaps the most pathetic instance of all was that of Robert Eaton, whose crime in 1757 was merely to have helped himself to someone else's rags in Chipping Norton. Almost certainly these were not first offences, however.

Transportation orders from Oxford can be identified for about 300 people between 1687 and 1775. Almost inevitably, perhaps, some were from the same family. The two William Whites may have been the first such in the 1680s; two men called Bailey (Henry and William) were also surely related, transported for the same crime of stealing shoes in Burford in 1737. In 1758 came the occurrence of a father and son, John Crook(e) senior and junior, both being sentenced to transportation for a theft at Wallingford. A few years later, two Thomas Gullivers, also likely to be a father and son, followed suit.* Both had originally been committed together on 8 October 1760 for the theft of some shirts at Fringford. The younger Gulliver was sentenced to seven years at the March 1761 assizes, but his father was discharged. It was a temporary reprieve. Both belonged to what *Jackson's Oxford Journal* called "the Bicester gang", the full extent of whose activities was revealed when one of their number, Joseph Westbury, provided King's evidence in December 1762. As a result of his revelations about the "iniquitous practices of this nest of villains", six men were charged with 18 robberies

---

* Probably either Thomas, the son of Edward, who was baptised on 1 April 1711, or Thomas, the son of Richard, baptised 10 November 1725. The younger Thomas was baptised as the son of Thomas and Mary on 25 September 1747 (all at Bicester).

committed over the previous few years. Gulliver was one of the six, and followed in his son's wake early in 1763, on the particular charge of stealing peas at Stoke Lyne, near Bicester. Westbury was discharged, care having been taken meanwhile to keep him separate from the rest of the gang "to prevent them from either tampering with him or doing him an injury".

While the recurrence of the same surnames over the century is suggestive of kinship, it is usually not possible to determine the exact relationship. Occasionally *Jackson's* settles any doubts. It exposed the cases of the brothers Charles and James Aris (or Ayris or Ayres) particularly well, for instance. Charles, a former "matross" (a soldier next in rank below the gunner in a train of artillery), had been transported for a theft recorded in *Jackson's* of 2 March 1765, when he stole sheets and other items from both the ostler's room of the Star Inn and the Wheatsheaf in Oxford. When he was spotted "marching off with his plunder in a sack", he dumped his haul and "took to his heels". Pursued with a cry of "Stop Thief!", he found himself in a cul-de-sac, so "made a double in the chace [sic] … and meeting his pursuers, pleaded his innocence". It was to no avail. He was taken thence to the city gaol, then to the castle, and soon after rather farther afield – albeit not for long. On 14 June 1766, *Jackson's* reported that Charles, or "Cagey" as he was known (implying presumably a man who was suspected of much, but admitted nothing), had "already finished his travels", having been spotted "in some of the most public parts" of Oxford. Very public indeed, if it was true that "he had the impudence to pay a visit to his brother, now a prisoner in our castle", an act of bravado which led *Jackson's* to suggest – not entirely accurately, as it turned out – that "he will soon find himself under a necessity of paying another visit to the same place".

The sibling in question, James, had been described as the brother of the "celebrated" Charles "Cagey" Aris when arrested in April 1766.* He was ordered for transportation for seven years for stealing iron bars from the palisades of a house in St Peter-in-the-East parish, the occupant of which had recently died. It was James Aris' bad luck that he had not been the first burglar to try to take advantage of the owner's demise, and the house was consequently being watched, with the result that he was caught in the act. His brother Charles was still at large when James was transported, and was tracked down only in November. At his trial in Reading in March the following year, Charles was given a temporary respite to allow "for enquiry into the validity of his defence, which was, that the ship in which he was embarked for the plantations was driven out of course by stress of weather, and that himself was forced on shore by the captain". He was not believed, however, and followed his brother in the summer of 1767, given a life sentence.

The first two obvious married couples to be transported from Oxford were contemporaries of the Aris brothers – although neither couple departed together, even though they were all implicated in the same crimes. Robert White was the first to go, transported in 1766 for a theft at Great Tew. The following year Mary Collett of Enstone followed suit, for the theft of a cloak in Witney. She had already experienced a stay in Witney's House of Correction in January 1766, classed as a vagrant for returning to the village of Great Tew from which she had already been once removed. Collett was accompanied on her journey overseas by John Keen (for stealing a cow) and Samuel Smith (for stealing a sheep), Thomas Hale (for

---

* These brothers seem certain to be James "Ayris" and Charles "Arise", both baptised at St Aldate's, in 1722 and 1734 respectively, the sons of John.

theft of bread in Shipton), and Sarah Cowell ("an incorrigible prostitute", whose seven years' sentence in America arose as a result of a short-lived escape from Thame Bridewell). *Jackson's* described the departure of the five prisoners "in high spirits" in its issue of 11 April 1767. A year later, Mary Collett's husband William followed. He had been found guilty of stealing gold rings and a piece of bacon in Enstone. One of the other four people dispatched with him, Hannah (the wife of Robert) White, had been found guilty of receiving Collett's stolen items. It is tempting to think that Collett (probably the man of that name baptised at Enstone on 24 April 1744) and White deliberately courted trouble in the hope of being reunited with their spouses on the other side of the Atlantic.*

The last order for American transportation issued by the Oxfordshire under-sheriff came in the summer of 1776. The convict in question was that double-escapologist Elizabeth Boswell (encountered in Chapter 2). The order was not carried out. America had ceased to be a viable destination, and, due to her elusiveness, Boswell was still on English soil at least until the summer of 1779. Not that transportation was inevitably a bad thing. For those who survived the voyage and whatever regime and climate awaited them, the New World could, with luck, offer attractive new opportunities. David Benfield, transported for theft in 1771, exemplifies the point. In a long letter printed in *Jackson's* of 5 December 1772 (see Figure 16) he positively revelled in letting his old associates back in Oxford know all about his changed fortunes.

---

* In 1758, another married couple, Richard and Mary Druet(t) or Drewett – who were married at Dorchester on 30 September 1745 – had been sentenced to 14 years' transportation for sheep-stealing. The orders for removal were prepared, but Richard died in prison before the sentence could be effected.

To Mr David Whitton at Bocardo
in the City of Oxford
with Speed   *Ingland*
Boltimore County Melaadys Manner, Mereland

Mr WHITTON

THIS Coms to a quaint you of my well fare and
the good and Bad fortin I have had since I
have been in a mericka I have had very Great Suc-
cefs in My undertakings I have folloed nothing but
phyfick & Surgorey since I have been heare I have
Don many Good and famus Cures in old wounds I
have Cured a boy that have been Lame for this 10
years and have and Cured many other that have
been lame for 2 or 3 years & have ben under all
the Surgions in this Cuntrey I have Cut 3 Cancers
~~out of the face and have cured them all~~

~~of Drugs I should be made for ever but I Dont~~
now any frind that old be so Good al tho it is in
my power to pay them as Soon as the Ship Returns
all my old a quaintans Livs neare me but are all
Sarvants which I Dont Ceep cumpany with for I
Keep the beft Cumpany as neare as I Can this yeare
I Shall yearn upwards of a hundred pound I Gives
20 pounds for my bord & horfes hay and Grafs I
find him Corn my self ——————————
Let it be fur or neare I allways Charge a Shilling a
mile for My Vifit I have Sent for 40 Miles but 20
often Sir I will Give you a Little a Count of the
Cuntrey the Cuntrey is fine and plefant Cyder uerey
plenty peaches and Chereys as plenty as the haw
bufhis bee in oxfordfhire partreg and fefants as
plenty as the Sparrows be in oxfordfhire all forts
of game are uerey plenty Likewife fifh flefh and
foul Chickins you may by for 2d purpees beef for
3 halfpence & mutton the fame I lives a bout 25
miles from boltimore found and bout 18 from Suf-
quana where Mr. Brickland Told me his brother
philip Lived I have inquired all as I cold and I heare
~~iflands to catch nozers~~

FIGURE 16 Extracts from David Benfield's ungrammatical and unpunctuated letter
from Maryland of 20 July 1772, reprinted in *Jackson's Oxford Journal* of 5 December 1772.

the Ship belonged to one Iacob Giles was Cold the
Elizabth pleaſt to Give My Kind Love to all your
brothers and Siſters and My old frind Mr Handrell
and Mrs Bew and Mr Wiſdoms and Mr Mears and
Mr Rollins Mrs Gadney and Mrs huſe and thair nai-
bor if you pleas that for Sworn Blackgard that Sore
hannah Cripſes pillabor which was Marked H C he
Swore the Each was em hee thoat to puniſh Me
but was miſtaken for I Lives Like a Ientieman and
hee Like a blackgard We have had a fine harveſt
as fine wheat as Can grow it is ſold for 4s & ſix
pence pur Buſhell I ſhall be uerey Glad to heare
from you to Let me Now how My naibors dos
pleaſt to Direct for Docter David Benfield to be Left
at Mr Jon Boyds Druggeſt in Boltimore Mereland
I Conclude with My Kind Love to yon and your
wife and my Little Bedflows Iane peggy and nan-
ney and am your Ever wellwiſher to Comand

    ye 20 Iuly 1772   D Benfield

             hare Brown is well &
Charls boſſom have got 2 Children and wife Iohn
brown have been married but his wife is Dead he
was Married to a Dutchwomman ho have Left him
a pees of Land Tobacco ſels in this Cuntrey for 15
Shilings pur hundred if I had a frind I Cold Ship
Tobacco. home but as I hant I Cant makeany thing
of marchandice I have 3 borders at 25 Shilings pur
month all with uerey bad wounds if Lee Elkington
had Com a Long with me hee Might a made him
Self for Ever for heare is Rabits as plenty as they
bee in a warren and make No youſe of the Skins a
tall and hats are uerey dear pleaſt to Give My Love
to Molly Carter & Mrs Bent and Carpenter I Shall
be might Glad to heare what is beCom of Lee I
beg of all Love in the world to Right to me to Let
me now how all my old frinds dos

       I Clude with My harty prayers for you and
am your D Benfield

            Rum is 2 shillings pur gallon
     pray Dont fail Righting pray excuſe my Scraul
for I am in haſt Luce bennet is a Live and well as
I heve heard but I hant ſeen She Mike is well hee
is Ceep by the County

"Partreg and fesants as plenty as the sparrows be in Oxfordshire": a letter from Maryland

-+>-<+-

The crime for which Benfield was transported was the theft of £40 and a silver tankard from the Crooked Billet in St Thomas' parish in June 1770. The items belonged to the landlord, Richard Crawford, and they were not all that he lost that day. In *Jackson's* of 16 June 1770 he placed a notice announcing his wife Mary's elopement the previous Tuesday (12th), renouncing responsibility for her behaviour or debts. He could have saved himself that further expense, because in the news column of the same issue it was reported that Mary Crawford and David Benfield had both already been committed to the city gaol.* Coincidence? Probably not, and it was presumably Benfield with whom she had hoped to elope. She was charged with assaulting her husband and "threatening to take away his life", poor Crawford having been "confined by a broken leg, which she had the cruelty to throw out of the box and displace the fractured bones". What happened to her is unknown, but Benfield was sentenced to seven years' transportation, probably on account of his previous record. He had been confined at the castle some years earlier for poaching deer, *Jackson's* observing ironically that he had been "extremely well known about the Royal Forest

---

* Crawford was from one of the half dozen or so families of St Thomas' which dominated the local river trade. According to Mary Prior's detailed genealogy in *Fisher Row*, Mary Crawford's maiden name must have been Kimber. Two members of the extended Crawford family were instrumental in the promulgation of the river rumour which resulted in the apprehension of the Abingdon waterturnpike murderers in 1790 – see Chapter 7.

of Whichwood, where his abilities will be long celebrated as an experienced practitioner".*

Although Benfield was sentenced in October 1770, it was not until the following summer that a vessel became available, and his letter, written only a year later, on 20 July 1772, provides a rare idea of what any transported man with enterprise might achieve. Addressed to Mr Whitton (David, by then dead, in fact), the keeper of the city gaol, Benfield's letter painted a picture of the "fine and pleasant" environs of Maryland almost impossible to imagine in class-ridden Georgian England, shivering in mid-winter. He wrote of the abundance of beef, mutton, fish, game, chickens, tobacco (which he was thinking of exporting), and rabbits; and of "as fine a harvest of wheat as can grow". In addition, the cider, peaches, and cherries were "as plenty as the haw bushes bee in Oxfordshire, partreg and fesants as plenty as the sparrows".

Most of the letter, however, is taken up with news of his own circumstances and those of some other former Oxford residents, "worthy characters", as *Jackson's* ironically called them, "of whom he makes honourable mention", namely:

- Lucy Bennett, the wife of Tobias, and daughter of a Worcester College butler called Smith. It was for stealing a silver spoon which was part of a much larger haul from the college that Bennett had been transported for seven years, in the summer of 1769.

- Charles Bossom, who had been sentenced to seven years' transportation at the quarter sessions of January 1763 for stealing "diverse pieces of butcher's meat" from Andrew Pearcy of

---

* Arthur Young, in *General View of Oxfordshire*, 1813, wrote of Wychwood that "the vicinity is filled with poachers, deer-stealers, thieves, and pilferers of every kind … and Oxford gaol would be uninhabited, were it not for this fertile source of crimes".

Oxford. Bossom was married with two children at the time of writing.*

- John Brown, sentenced to seven years for stealing poultry in Oxford in 1760, and of whom it was said by Benfield that he had inherited property from his Dutch wife after she died.

- Henry (spelled 'Hare') Brown, sentenced to seven years in October 1769 for stealing a fowl from Mrs Chillingworth of Oxford. He had escaped once from the city gaol in March 1770, "in the absence of the gaoler by forcing the keys from his daughter", but to no avail. According to *Jackson's*, Brown, "being betrayed by the clinking of his fetters as he ran through the streets, was retaken near Wadham College".

Benfield provided news of one other person with Oxford connections in "a mericka". But Philip Brickland (probably the brother of William Brickland, an Oxford teacher) was there out of choice – and the news was less cheerful. He was the captain of a slave ship called the *Elizabeth* and had secured a large number of slaves on a trip "to the islands". He was not expected to return, though, because other "negors roas and got a board and cruely used all the ships cru after whipped them all most to death then hanged them and burnt the ship after releasing all the slaves".†

A number of Benfield's old Oxford acquaintances are also addressed in his letter. These include David Whitton's wife,

---

* Bossom is another St Thomas' name inseparable from the history of Oxford's waterways. According to Peter Wilson Coldham in *King's Passengers to Maryland and Virginia* (1997), by 1798 Bossom owned 143 acres of land in Baltimore. William Bossom, another member of the family (whose wider influence is described in *A Towpath Walk in Oxford*), had been ordered for transportation in 1768.

† Benfield concludes this sobering news with the comment that a slave could fetch 70 or 80 pounds in Maryland – making slaves a far more profitable cargo than transports, whose value was suppressed on account of their normally finite period of service.

brothers, and sisters, "Mr. Wisdoms" (meaning Charles, the county gaoler, presumably), Hannah "Cripse"* (whose property Benfield seems also to have been accused of stealing), and Lee Elkington (an Oxford hatter sentenced to transportation in January 1771, but whose sentence, on account of his youth, was commuted to service in the Navy).

David Benfield had either learned or pre-possessed rudimentary medical skills. This undoubtedly made his lot in America much more pleasant than for many. Nonetheless, news of a man who could claim within a year of banishment to expect to earn some 100 pounds that year was no doubt cheering indeed in the chill of a British winter for any convicts about to make the long journey themselves. Cheering too for Sir John Fielding (of Bow Street), should he ever have heard of it. In 1773 he called transportation "the wisest, because most humane and effectual, punishment we have" on the basis that it "immediately removes the evil, separates the individual from his abandoned connections, and gives him a fresh opportunity of being a useful member of society". Benfield's was an excellent case in favour of his argument.† Not that many Oxford prisoners subsequently had the chance to test Fielding's theory or the accuracy of Benfield's account. The last major exodus occurred towards the end of 1774, bound for a ship at Bristol again for the first time since 1723, as far as can be told. After that, the stirrings of American rebellion made transportation

---

* Probably the Hannah Cripps "from the castle" who was buried at St Thomas' on 13 September 1769.

† Coldham, in *King's Passengers* (1997), summarises Benfield's will, which was proved on 17 May 1779. There he identified his wife (in America, presumably) as Hannah, his father-in-law as Thomas Elliott, and his mother as Mary. His brother William was living at Great Barrington, near Burford, with a wife Mary and son David. One of the witnesses was John Brown.

much less feasible. The usual alternative, for a decade or more, was to apply forced labour rather closer to home.

Hard labour on the Thames

→>-<←

The first known Oxfordshire men sentenced to hard labour specifically on the Thames were the brothers Thomas and William Smith. They had been tried at the assizes of July 1776 for robbing Henry Harrison of Trinity College of nine guineas and a watch on the highway near Witney. As so often happened, they were reprieved from the death penalty, in this case on condition that they enlist for military service in the East Indies, "never more to be at large again in this kingdom". Their application was refused, however, and the rather more convenient (and lenient) sentence of six years' labour on the Thames was applied. Accordingly they were accommodated on board a hulk in Woolwich, which was as far afield as many criminals who might otherwise have been transported went for the next few years. The two brothers were housed on board the *Justitia* (a former trans-Atlantic transportation vessel) in December 1776; another hulk frequently used to accommodate felons from Oxford was the *Censor*. However, it was the *Tayloe* on which one of the most charismatic, and yet enigmatic, of all of Oxford Castle's thousands of inmates was confined. His name was Peter le Maitre, whose particular notoriety and mystique stems from the suggestion that he either reinvented himself, or actually always was, the French revolutionary Jean Paul Marat (1749–1793).

Le Maitre, described as both a Swiss hairdresser and French teacher of drawing, had been in Oxford since at least August 1775, as it was then that his wife announced in *Jackson's* that her tambour business (a newly devised form of embroidery) had relocated to the Cornmarket. Assuring her customers of unsurpassed "neatness of work and elegancy of pattern", she also offered "lessons in tambour". Accounts of the circumstances leading to the robbery vary, but it seems that le Maitre had ingratiated himself with the supervisors of the old Ashmolean Museum, and within a short time was permitted to study the exhibits unsupervised.* It was misplaced trust, and in February 1776, when the museum found itself bereft of numerous golden coins, medals, and chains valued at nearly £200, he was quickly identified as the culprit. His method had been to hide beneath a staircase at closing time, enabling him to escape with his booty after dark.

A Bow Street notice in the *General Evening Post* (17–20 February 1776) described le Maitre as: "a short thin man, squints very much, marked with the small-pox, stoops a little, has black hair … two tambour waistcoats, a scarlet coat, and a French grey coat". Going first to London, then East Anglia, he then made his way to Dublin, but was arrested by the Irish authorities and brought back to Oxford under *habeas corpus* in September. It would be six months before the trial, and meanwhile le Maitre put his time to productive use. In *Jackson's* of 16 November 1776 he announced the first issue of an intended monthly autobiographical publication entitled "The Wanderer and Unfortunate Husband; or the Life, Adventures and Travels of Peter le Maitre". Claiming to counter the "ridiculous and false" tales then circulating, le Maitre expressed the cajoling hope that "the truth will not appear altogether void of charms, nor the adventures he takes upon himself to relate, the

---

* This was not the current Ashmolean, which adopted the name only in 1899, but Elias Ashmole's collection in its original location, now the University Museum of the History of Science in Broad Street.

less pleasing for being within reach of probability". Subscribers were advised to call at the castle or apply at his house near the back gate of Exeter College, where, presumably, his (equally "unfortunate"?) wife was in residence. At the trial in March 1777, le Maitre represented himself. He attempted to defend himself on several counts, including that he had been given the missing items by a member of the University in lieu of a debt. This proving to be clearly a lie, the judge seemed to take as dim a view of this "horrid insinuation" against an Oxford gentleman as he did of the crime itself, and pronounced a sentence of five years' hard labour on the Thames. Consequently le Maitre was conveyed to the *Tayloe* hulk on 15 April.

In the short intervening period between the trial and his removal, it is perhaps not surprising that a man as resourceful and inventive as le Maitre should have attempted to escape. This was the era of Solomon Wisdom, after all, when it seems to have been almost *de rigeur* to attempt at least one breakout. Four other men were implicated in the failed effort of early April, one being the wounded but resilient highwayman, John Jones, who evidently treated this experience as practice for his successful break-out of a little less than a year later (as described in Chapter 3). *Jackson's* reported that the men had used faggot sticks and a clamp from a pump to undermine a wall in the felons' apartment, where there was a drain which had formerly been a doorway. They disposed of the spoil down "the necessary" (i.e. the toilet), but their plan was discovered when one of the mats which covered the hole was moved, revealing tell-tale signs of daylight. They had subsequently been handcuffed and more closely confined (*Jackson's* 5 April 1777). Le Maitre was moved to the *Tayloe* hulk on account of the lack of any suitable transportation destination, but the scarcity of surviving records relating to the Thames hulks means that his ultimate fate will probably always remain a mystery.*

After the Treaty of Paris in September 1783 some attempts were made to resurrect the practice of American transportation. Equally, some attempts were made to avoid the journey right up to the last moment! In May 1784, *Jackson's* carried two items in relation to a mass escape from a transportation vessel called the *Great Duke of Tuscany* near Torbay. Seven Oxfordshire criminals were among 25 who were quickly rearrested. These were (with ages taken from the July 1783 Calendar of Prisoners) 28-year-old John Baughan (a cabinet maker from Asthall, near Burford), William Bowler, Edward Harris, Samuel Hussey, Matthew Mills (20), Thomas Turner, and Richard Wingate, alias "West Country Dick" (55). All seven were among the 22 men whose departure from Oxford had been noted in *Jackson's* of 20 March 1784. Three others were William Best, Paul Ragg, and James Slatford (encountered in Chapter 3).† With more than one hundred individuals from various parts of the country at large, the Devon authorities were stretched to the limit. Consequently, Solomon Wisdom and a turnkey were summoned to Exeter to help with identification. None of the above was named among the ringleaders, who were given capital sentences, albeit then commuted on a point of law. The episode created a considerable delay and resulted in complete change of destination for Baughan,

---

* Le Maitre's crime and true identity are discussed in two scholarly articles in the *English Historical Review*: "The Robbery from the Ashmolean Museum, 1776" (1931) and "Le Maitre, alias Marat" (1934), the author J. M. Thompson concluding that: "The impartial historian can only record a verdict of Not Proven". Marat was responsible for the massacres of many Royalist sympathisers in Paris prisons in 1792, and was murdered himself in 1793.
† Only in the years 1783 and 1784 do the Oxford Calendars of Prisoners specify a destination. Ragg, Slatford, and a prisoner called Thomas Jobson (alias Johnson) are consistently noted as destined for Africa, but another nine always for America (presumably Nova Scotia, which remained loyal to the British cause).

Hussey, Turner, and Mills, all of whom departed on 13 May 1787 on the *Friendship* as part of the "First Fleet" bound for the new penal colony of Botany Bay.

Hard labour in Oxford

→>-<←

From March 1785, although the sentence of transportation was often recorded against a prisoner's name, this seems consistently to have resulted in rather the opposite, with the individual never venturing more than a mile or two from his cell. The British authorities may have assumed that the system of transportation would revert seamlessly after the American war, but it was not to be, and Oxford was anyway quick to realise the folly of expelling a convenient and cheap labour force when there was plenty of work to be done at home – in two senses of the word: "at home" being a cant term among criminals for "in prison".* As the physical reconstruction of the prison buildings began, who better to provide the labour than the prisoners themselves? Some were obviously so employed until a suitable transportation vessel became available, or until the number of prisoners exceeded the available space, or indeed until the very work in which they were engaged compromised their own security. In April 1786, for instance, *Jackson's* stated that three prisoners were conveyed early to a hulk at Woolwich to await onward transportation to Africa. This was not because a suitable vessel had been located, but because of the insecure nature of the castle gaol, "which is considerably weakened by the demolition of some of

---

* When the horse-thief James Williams (see Chapter 6) was tracked down in May 1790, *Jackson's* announced that he had been discovered "in the thieves' phrase, *at home*, being in Clerkenwell prison".

The following ſtatement clearly proves the benefit of the ſyſtem purſued in the County of Oxford, with re-ſpeᶜt to the management of the Priſoners under con-finement, and ſentenced to hard labour, within that County. The number of Priſoners, beſides thoſe con-fined for a ſhort Time, between the iſt of January, 1794, and the iſt of January, 1795, was only nineteen, and the following is a ſtatement of their coſt and their earnings : —

				£	s.	d.
County Allowance of Bread.	-	·		35	0	9
N. B. This Expence muſt have been incurred if the Priſoners had not been employed in hard Labour.						
Extra Food and Clothing,	-	-	-	27	2	8
Overlooker,	-	-	-	23	8	0
Expence in Tools,	-	-		3	2	0
Expence of Hire of Horſes and Carts on the Botley Road,	-	-	-	3	6	0
Total Expence,				£ 91	19	5
Earnings of Priſoners at the Caſtle Works,		-		£ 78	5	1
Work done on the Canal Navigation,		-		13	11	0
Done on the River Navigation,		-	-	5	14	6
Sawing Stone,	-	-	-	15	10	8
For keeping the Botley Road in repair,		-		12	12	0
Total Earnings,	-	-		125	13	3
Total Expence,	-	-		91	19	5
Balance,	-	-		£ 33	13	10

It is to be noted, that the Overlooker having ſo few Conviᶜts to take care of, was almoſt conſtantly employed in the reſpeᶜtive Works with the Priſoners.

PRICE of STOCKS.

Bank Stock, ſhut	Long Ann. ſhut
Five per Cent. 94 ¾	India Stock, ——
Four per Ct. Con. ſhut	India Bonds, 1 Diſ.
Three per Ct. Con. 62 ⅝	Navy and Viᶜt. Bills, 4 Diſ.

ADVERTISEMENTS *omitted this Week, will appear in our next.*

FIGURE 17 The earnings and expenses of the prisoners at hard labour at the castle, and on the canal, the river, and the Botley Road, as printed in *Jackson's Oxford Journal* of 28 March 1795.

the exterior walls, and is now rebuilding with great improvements and upon a very extensive plan". Two of these three were Thomas Gearing (42) and William Marriner (23), both accomplices to Miles Ward, who had been executed the previous month (see Chapter 8). Neither man reached Africa, finding themselves instead aboard the *Alexander,* one of the "First Fleet" vessels which departed on 13 May 1787, although Gearing did not survive the voyage.

It was Daniel Harris, still Clerk of Works, under whom this "extensive plan" was being effected, but by the end of the year, partly on account of the "Daniel Damnable" incident (described in Chapter 2), he would assume sole command. Under his assured authority, the practicality of using prison labour became still more viable, and specific sentences of "hard labour in the Castle works" became common, the first such being in the Calendar of Prisoners for 7 March 1787.

Simultaneously, the enlightened change from seeing a prison as a place of actual or impending punishment to regarding it as one of improvement is evident. A fund for establishing "pecuniary rewards to be distributed amongst convicts and prisoners at their discharge, as shall have conducted themselves to the satisfaction" of the magistrates was established. It was funded by subscription, but was soon unnecessary, as the value of the labour provided by the prisoners proved sufficient in itself. By the end of 1787, the fund had a balance of £113 9s 2d, after all expenses were paid, and no further private contributions were required.

By the end of 1791, the prisoners' efforts "within the walls … on the River Navigation and the repair of the Botley Turnpike road" earned a balance of £115 7s 11d, after deducting the costs of their "clothing and maintenance". The comparison was made between this figure and the £122 16s 7d that the county would have had to pay anyway as bread allowance even had the prisoners remained idle. Reporting this in its issue of 18 February 1792, *Jackson's* also took the opportunity to emphasise the wider social benefits, saying

> it is here proper to observe that this mode of recalling the prisoners to habits of labour seems the most rational means of rendering them useful members of society by their future industry, in confirmation of which, several of those already discharged have been since employed in places of some trust, and have hitherto acquitted themselves entirely to the satisfaction of their employers.

It was the same story for at least the next few years, as the demand for labour at the castle, on the Thames and Oxford Canal, and on other public works continued unabated (see Figure 17). Oxford therefore has much reason to be thankful to these eighteenth-century felons, who were in turn probably themselves thankful not to be labouring in the southern hemisphere, once the route to Australia had become a feasible option in 1787. Some might actually have preferred such a fate, however: debtors, for instance, faced with the utterly demoralising prospect of incarceration with meagre sustenance and no fixed date for the expiration of their sentence …

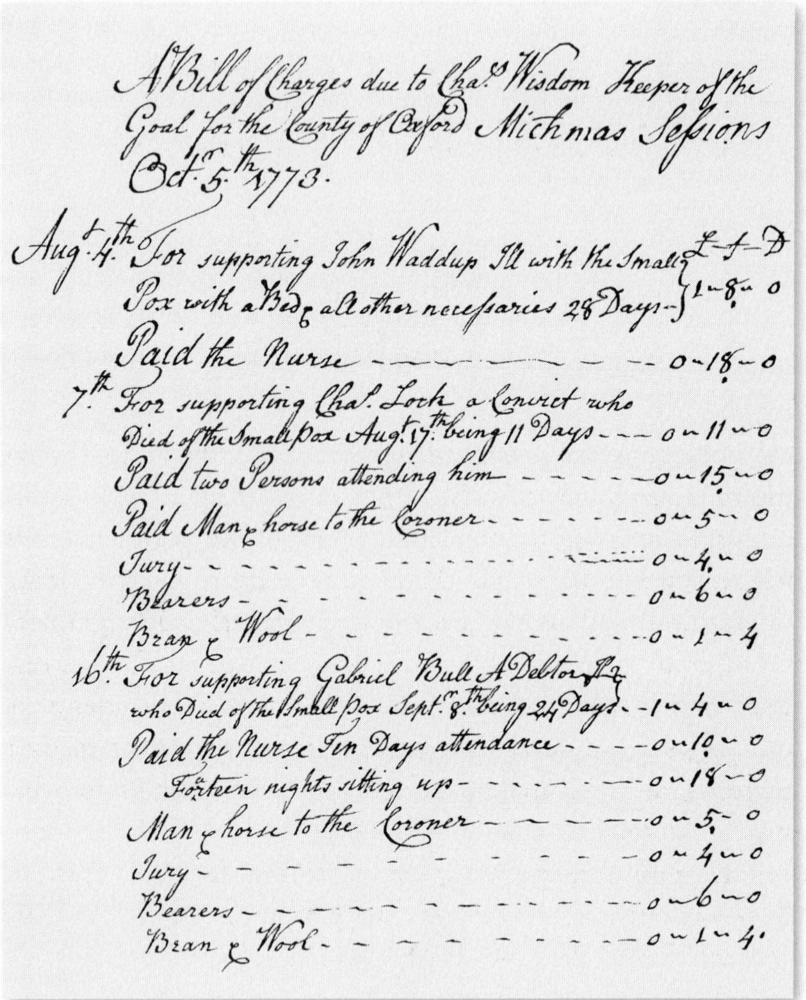

A Bill of Charges due to Chas. Wisdom Keeper of the Goal for the County of Oxford Michmas Sessions Oct. 5th 1773.

		£ – s – D
Aug. 4th	For supporting John Waddup Ill with the Small Pox with a Bed & all other necessaries 28 Days	1 – 8 – 0
	Paid the Nurse	0 – 18 – 0
7th	For supporting Chas. Lock a Convict who Died of the Small Pox Aug. 17th being 11 Days	0 – 11 – 0
	Paid two Persons attending him	0 – 15 – 0
	Paid Man & horse to the Coroner	0 – 5 – 0
	Jury	0 – 4 – 0
	Bearers	0 – 6 – 0
	Bran & Wool	0 – 1 – 4
16th	For supporting Gabriel Bull A Debtor &c who Died of the Small Pox Sept. 8th being 24 Days	1 – 4 – 0
	Paid the Nurse Ten Days attendance	0 – 10 – 0
	Fourteen nights sitting up	0 – 18 – 0
	Man & horse to the Coroner	0 – 5 – 0
	Jury	0 – 4 – 0
	Bearers	0 – 6 – 0
	Bran & Wool	0 – 1 – 4

FIGURE 18 Charles Wisdom's bill of Michaelmas 1773 for the costs of nursing some of the many smallpox sufferers of that year, and the funerals of two of them: Charles Lock, a felon due for transportation, and Gabriel Bull, a debtor. Lock was buried at St Thomas' Church. [*Copyright: Oxfordshire History Centre*]

CHAPTER FIVE

DEBTORS, DONORS, DEATHS, AND DISEASES

The eighteenth-century prisoners in Oxford Castle were consistently identified as either felons (that is, convicts) or debtors, accommodated in separate parts of the prison. Debtors fell into two broad categories. Some – enterprising, law-abiding citizens on the whole, no doubt, whose only real fault might have been greed or naivety – were imprisoned specifically for that civil offence; some, however, were indebted as a direct result of incarceration for some other misdemeanour, finding themselves subsequently unable to pay the fine or the accumulated gaoler's fees required to obtain release.

Take John Staite, for instance, during his first spell of imprisonment for clipping coins (see Chapter 4). In *The Cry of the Oppressed* (1691) the prisoner Thomas Hill recorded in November 1690 that "Staytt", as he wrote the name, "was forced to tick in the celler [sic] at his first coming; they have run him up six pounds". The cellar was evidently a place of relative luxury, but at a cost, and although Staite had found the means to pay off some of this bill, he "remains prisoner for three pounds due to the celler, and has been so six months". He "desired to lie in the tower, or dungeon, that so he might be rent-free, but the mistress of the prison" [i.e. Mrs Thorpe] refused, and "so forces him to that vast expense of a bed, that so poor man he may continue a prisoner all his life time". That did not happen, of course, although Staite failed to learn from this experience, and was subsequently transported after convictions for two other crimes.

The absurdity of this way of treating debtors was highlighted in 1729 by Colonel James Oglethorpe (who became the founder and first governor of the transportation colony of Georgia in 1732).* He induced Parliament to enquire into the horrors of the debtors' prisons in London. The practice of franchising prisons to gaolers whose income depended almost exclusively on what could be extracted from the prisoners was standard. This meant that it was not uncommon for a gaoler to torture debtors, occasionally even to death, in vain attempts to extract fees from men who by the very nature of their situation had no money to give. There is no evidence that Oxford's debtors received treatment of this severity, although occasional hints do appear of victimisation, deprivation, and possible misappropriation of even the meagre relief which was, in times of dire want, sometimes granted. Under these circumstances some men (and debtors almost always were men) spent a very long time indeed inside the castle, with little hope of repaying the debt, and no means of support other than the charity of others.

---

* Oglethorpe was an alumnus of Corpus Christi College. His Secretary in Georgia for part of 1736 was Charles Wesley (1707–1788), founder of the Methodist Church with his brother John (1703–1791). The two men were regular visitors to Oxford Castle Gaol in the 1730s, attempting to teach many prisoners to read and to find work, and sometimes paying off debts.

Thomas Salmon:
baker of Bicester

-+>-<+-

One common way for a debtor to raise funds was to appeal
to neighbours. This is what Thomas Salmon, a Bicester baker,
requested permission to do in 1725. It is not clear how he came
to be in debt, but one suspects from some earlier correspondence
that his penury may to some extent have been self-inflicted, by
being just a little too critical of men who had the power to affect
his reputation and therefore his custom. In April 1718 he had been
committed to prison for denouncing without proof four Bicester
families as traitors, and for failing to produce anyone willing to act
as sureties for his subsequent good behaviour. Early in 1720 he faced
further charges on account of a threatening letter sent to Samuel
Trotman of Bucknell, the magistrate responsible for his earlier
arrest. Salmon, evidently, was a man of many words, not all of them
judicious, and his case is a good illustration of the ramifications of
indebtedness for a man's immediate family. By January 1725, he had
already been in prison for 57 weeks, dependent solely on whatever
"meagre sustenance" his wife could provide. Now even that would
be denied him, as it had "pleased God to visit his family with the
smallpox, his house to be fired, his wife burnt and lamed, and his
goods to be seized". To add further pathos, Salmon also alluded to
the resultant suffering of his three children, the youngest being only
29 weeks old.* Despite all his woes, it would seem that his heartfelt
request to be allowed to seek the charity of his neighbours failed,

---

* Debtors were, it would seem, allowed conjugal relations during visits by their spouses!
Only one baptism of any child of Thomas Salmon is apparent at Bicester, in 1717.

because even though the Oxfordshire records relating to debtors are patchy, it was not until the Lent assizes of 1736 that Salmon was "discharged by proclamation". Good for him, you might think, but no, the conclusion of this particularly melancholy tale came less than a month later with the wretched man's burial at Bicester on 7 April 1736.

Salmon's incarceration coincided with that of a man whose familiarity with Oxford Castle was second only to that of the keepers. Indeed, Marshall Tims of Hook Norton could probably boast a rather superior knowledge, since whereas each member of the Etty family who ran the prison successively in the first third of the eighteenth century did so for only a few a years, Tims was there, off and on, for the best part of three decades!

"An incorrigible rogue": Marshall Tims of Hook Norton

++>-<+-

Tims' name first appears in a quarter sessions petition for bread at Easter 1722, by when he might well already have been in the castle for some time. He had been released by 1724, because he was apprehended in September that year at the turnpike gate at Yarnton in possession of a basket containing seven hares, a rabbit, and a bullet mould. In April 1725 Tims' troubles began in earnest, when he committed an assault on Thomas Freeman of Ditchley (near Charlbury). For failing to pay the resulting fine, he was sent to Witney Bridewell; for failing to resist the temptation to break out of it, he was sentenced to three months at Oxford Castle. This sentence commenced early in 1727, on the basis of his being "an incorrigible rogue and setting snares in Mixbury warren" (near

Brackley, Northants.). But his real problem was his inability to pay his fine, or to find anyone willing to commit to a surety that he would keep the peace with his old foe Thomas Freeman. You can see why. Having somehow found the means to engineer his release by the end of 1727, Tims was soon in trouble again for further assaults, this time on John Minchin of Hook Norton in October 1727 and on Henry Bunting of Cassington in March the following year. Again, understandably, no-one was willing to vouch for his good behaviour, so he spent the next two and a half years, between Michaelmas 1729 and Trinity 1732, detained at the castle "for sureties and to prosecute his traverses". Again in 1733 he found the means for release, and again he lost little time in re-offending, receiving a six-month sentence for shooting at his old adversary John Minchin. The sentence presumably served, he was back yet again the following year on two counts, a prosecution brought against him by, intriguingly, the Duke of Argyle (for trespass, and not for the first time), and for failure to pay a fine of £10 for a further assault on Henry Bunting. And there, from 1734 on, Tims remained for an incredible further 14 years until the summer of 1748.

You might have thought that a man who had spent the best part of 30 years in prison would have learned his lesson, but no, not Tims, who was back inside once more by the October of 1749! John Dawson of Heythrop (near Enstone) was the latest person with whom Tims had fallen out, having threatened him "whereby he is in danger of his life". His case was considered remarkable enough at the time for the Reading newspaper the *Oxford Gazette & Reading Mercury* to allocate a little of the tiny proportion of its pages that it devoted to local news to announce that on Tuesday 5 September Tims had been sent back to prison "for want of security for his appearance" at the next quarter sessions, "the peace being sworn against him by one John Dawson, servant to the Right Honourable the Earl of Shrewsbury". The paper went on to add, only slightly inaccurately: "It is remarkable that the said Tims was dischar'd at Trinity Sessions 1748, after lying in gaol 21 years for a fine pass'd on him for a fact of the same nature." The date of his final release is not clear, but Tims did apparently behave himself after this, to be buried at Great Tew in October 1767.

Apparently incapable of curbing his temper, Tims may indeed have truly been the "incorrigible rogue" that the justices dubbed him, who then fell foul of the law of debt by failing to pay the resultant costs. Many debtors were of a very different ilk, however, as their elegantly composed petitions for alms show. Thomas Salmon of Bicester was a case in point; Thomas Moulden, a peruke (periwig) maker and barber from Witney, was another.

Thomas Moulden of Witney:
imprisoned "not for debt, theft nor defraud"
→►◄←

Moulden's case is illuminated by the opportunity that he took to air his grievances through a medium not available to his predecessors: *Jackson's Oxford Journal* (which was first published in 1753 – see Appendix 5). In a series of notices placed in the newspaper between 1776 and 1779, Moulden expressed eloquently the hopeless situation of many debtors, even though his own circumstances were not at all typical. In September 1776, soon after his imprisonment, the 65-year-old placed his first notice, claiming that he was in prison solely because an Oxfordshire attorney had cheated him of his rightful estate. Consequently he offered the rights to that estate to anyone able "to avenge his case, free him from prison, and allow him a subsistence for life". There were evidently no takers, since a similar appeal appeared in the paper in January 1778, reiterating Moulden's claim to have been wrongfully imprisoned, "not for debt, theft nor defraud", but as a victim of fraud himself. This time he identified Mr John Jones of Wichcombe (sic) as the manipulating attorney in question, and the disputed estate as "Moulden's Wood" in the parish of Ducklington. This, he claimed, "was taken from him by violence after he had been in possession five years". His offer now was a £300 reward for anyone who could help him to "recover his birthright" and provide charity to help him to survive in the meantime.

Thus far one's sympathy lies with Moulden, an intelligent man, evidently, who had apparently been unjustifiably incarcerated for well over a year. But two weeks after he divulged Jones' name, *Jackson's* published a response from "Verax" of Witney, which gave another side to the story. Moulden, it seems, had been given every opportunity some years earlier to prove in court his right to the estate, but had failed to do so. It was because he had been unable to pay the resultant costs that he had suffered an earlier period of imprisonment, and a second one when he was later apprehended cutting down timber in the wood that he so obviously considered to be his own. This had obliged the owner to bring an action for damages, and it was this – Moulden's second failure to pay either compensation or costs – that was the cause of his current detention.*

---

* In *Jackson's* of 9 and 23 May 1772 Moulden is named among debtors intending to take advantage of a new Insolvency Act. He had then been at the castle since at least the summer of 1771, and was presumably successful, since he was summoned again at Easter 1773, designated then as a barber, for cutting down 50 oak and 50 hazel trees in Edgeley Coppice, a part of Moulden's Wood.

The notices subsequently placed by Moulden made no further reference to his claim, but concentrated on his own deteriorating circumstances. By July 1779, approaching the end of the third year of his current sentence at the gaol, he had sold all his effects, and was reduced to begging to avoid starving. It did the trick! Half a guinea was contributed, he informed *Jackson's* readers in his next instalment two weeks later, but sadly, as he had had no allowance whatsoever since the end of June, this was insufficient. A further £3 was what he needed "to supercede out of" prison. He concluded:

> I humbly beg and pray the charitable and humane to consider my truly miserable and unhappy circumstance, and afford me such relief as they shall think most meet, to help me out of my distress, and I will, as in duty bound, ever pray.

Gone was the offer of a lucrative share in a valuable estate – benefactors would have to be content merely with Moulden's prayers now! – but that was sufficient for some: by October he had reached his target, thanks to a single gift of three guineas from a unknown lady. Unfortunately, this had still proved inadequate, as he was now being prevented from leaving, so he claimed, by his own attorney (to whom, by implication, he was also in debt). As a result, Moulden said, "I have no friend, nor can I help myself, and must inevitably starve without relief, which is what they aim at."

This imagined intention of his adversaries may well have been achieved, in fact, since Thomas Moulden did not live much longer, being buried (as Thomas "Moulder") at Witney in September 1781. Whether he was a genuinely wronged man or an obsessive fantasist is difficult to tell, but the wood *had* certainly once belonged to the Moulden family. A Witney ironmonger called Edward Moulden

(?–1713) had purchased it in 1693.* The baptisms of eight of
Edward's children were registered at Witney between 1676 and
1686, but there was no subsequent baptism there of any boy called
Thomas. The implication is that Thomas, whether truly a relative
or not, convinced himself that, simply because the wood carried
his surname, he was its rightful owner. Whatever, even though he
never did prove his case, it would seem that his persistence may
have paid off in some way, since the woodland to the south-west
of Ducklington does, surprisingly perhaps, still commemorate the
family's name: labelled "Mouldings Wood" on the first Ordnance
Survey map, surveyed in 1830–33, today it continues to be designated
"Moulden's Wood".

Thomas Moulden aired his grievances with an impressive degree
of sophistication, and exposed the unhappy situation of many
debtors with convincing erudition. It was the situation of prisoners
such as the Witney barber and peruke-maker whom John Howard
had in mind when campaigning to abolish prisoners' gaol fees
by paying a salary to the keeper. Howard made his first visits to
Oxford Castle in 1773 and 1774, and on his return on Christmas
Day 1782 it was apparent that any progress since the publication of
the first edition of *State of the Prisons in England and Wales* in 1777
had been slow. Fifteen of the 31 felons of both sexes had actually
been discharged, but were being retained as a result of the ludicrous
ramifications of a system which – even though Solomon Wisdom
did in fact receive a salary of £20 a year – required inmates with no

---

* The successive owners of the wood are detailed in the *Victoria County History* for
Bampton Hundred. Part of Moulden's Wood had been purchased by the wealthy
Harcourt family in about 1754, but not Edgeley Coppice, which had probably been
sold off by Edward Moulden long before – something Thomas Moulden may have
failed to comprehend. The next named owners are the Leake family, at the end of the
eighteenth century.

source of income to pay their bills before being allowed to leave. Yet the prisoners at Oxford were probably generally more fortunate than their peers elsewhere in the country, in at least being able to benefit from the generosity of the liberal minds and purses that characterised a university city like Oxford.

Prison charities and "the most expressive effusions of reverence and gratitude"

-+>-<+-

John Howard described the principal prison charities existing in Oxford in 1777. Thomas Horde's Charity was the best-established. Horde, who had been "confined here for some offence against government" (in the 1680s), paid for the chapel (see Figures 4 and 5) and bequeathed an annual sum of £14 to pay for a chaplain, plus the same sum for distribution among the prisoners, both debtors and felons. Horde altered this provision in August 1709 to a legacy of £2 a month solely for the prisoners. But by 1777 the estates from which this income was derived (one being a property in Cote, near Bampton) were able to produce only 33 shillings a month, "which was paid by the rector of Lincoln College, and is now paid by the principal of Trinity, who are always two of the twelve trustees".

The other dual-purpose funds were a somewhat miserly 8s 8d per quarter from Magdalen College, plus 40 shillings every Lent, "commonly called *forfeit-money*", and the following:

> Debtors have in common every Saturday six pounds of mutton sent by a gentleman of Christ church college. From two other colleges they have in bread about 2s a week. Christ church and New college send them broth, generally three times in a fortnight.

Yet even this sustenance came at a price, Howard adding that "the prisoners pay four pence to the man who brings it". That comment immediately raises doubts about how much of these displays of benevolence by concerned Oxford individuals and institutions found its way to its intended beneficiaries. Certainly (as seen in Chapter 1), the quarter sessions records are peppered with imploring appeals from desperate inmates. Often they pleaded for food or clothing; occasionally they alleged neglect, but it is difficult to discern much criticism of the keepers of the gaols themselves. That could be because the Oxford gaolers were more humane than many of their counterparts elsewhere; but it could also represent simple diplomacy. It is very risky to point the finger at someone who has complete power over you. Sometimes the risk was considered worth taking. The debtor David Gadsdon spoke out during the dramatic events leading to the appointment of Daniel Harris in 1786 (see Chapter 2), for instance; and in 1763 Thomas Harris, Richard Barton, John Whitton (who was transported in the same year), John Ansell, and Thomas Parry claimed that "the charity money left to the prisoners by Mr. Horde has not been paid to us for this thirteen months past". Whether this represented a failure by the trustees or misappropriation by William Wisdom is not clear, but there must have been considerable opportunity for the gaoler to cream off alms intended for the prisoners. The gaolers submitted their bills for the cost of food, nursing, funerals, and so on only every quarter – long enough, probably, for many irregularities to go unnoticed.*

And if the gaoler did somehow divert alms for his own personal

---

* Conversely, some keepers showed compassion beyond their brief. In their meeting of Trinity 1734 the magistrates agreed to reimburse Elizabeth Etty for looking after a poor woman who "came accidentally to ye castle being very ill with a miscarege".

gain, he was not the only one! Sometimes, the money failed to get even that far. It was left to the deprived prisoners themselves to notify the public in *Jackson's* of 11 January 1766 that "two men carrying a poor's box have begged about under pretence of asking charity for us, but no money so collected has been brought, and therefore they must have been impostors". However, this was an exception, and the pages of *Jackson's* show that help did regularly reach its intended recipients. In 1773, for instance, something unprecedented happened when a charity set up to provide bread for the poor of the city agreed to allocate its surplus of £3 3s 2d to Rev. Swinton, the long-serving prison chaplain, to buy bread for the prisoners. Swinton also remembered his former charges when he died in 1777, leaving a bequest of £100 from which a sum should

> weekly be laid out in the purchase of bread to be distributed amongst the prisoners in Oxford Castle as should constantly attend divine service, the same to be distributed by the minister attending the said prison, and the keeper of the said prison for the time being allotting to each of them a threepenny loaf till the whole should be expended.

In 1775, another clergyman, Rev. John Cox of St Giles', also made a gift to be divided among the prisoners at the castle. But then, as his prayers had been answered with an extraordinary lottery prize of £5,000, he could afford to be generous!

In 1776, a group of prisoners adopted an unusual means of raising funds. *Jackson's* of 27 January 1776 reported that they had erected in the courtyard "an edifice composed entirely of snow, representing the gothic arch and entrance to a cave". The observation that this "curious construction … has already attracted the attention of good numbers" suggests that the prisoners had spied an opportunity to seek donations from people with whom they might otherwise never have had contact. No doubt *Jackson's* very mention of it would have attracted still more "good numbers" soon after.

In the 1780s, numerous notices of appeal and thanks from the prisoners testify to the slowness with which John Howard's recommendations were being implemented. Public thanks was given to Queen's, Oriel, and New Colleges in 1782 and 1783, for instance, and on 3 January 1784, 80 prisoners (26 of whom were debtors) expressed their gratitude to Worcester, Queen's, and Jesus Colleges in addition to many named individuals. Later that year, the newspaper championed the prisoners' cause of its own volition, stating on 14 February 1784:

> there being no gaol allowance of any kind for the debtors, and bread only for the felons, some of whom, we find, have suffered confinement near two years since their respective trials, notwithstanding the repeated applications of the bench of justices. Hence it will easily be credited that some of them are almost destitute of apparel; to whom any kind of cast-off clothes would be highly acceptable. The keeper we learn has lately been under a necessity of destroying the old matting etc on which the felons slept, in order to relieve them from loathsome vermin, and bed coverings of all kinds are become exceedingly scarce.

Another winter, another appeal. On 11 December 1784 the prisoners, in their own words, requested help "to alleviate their present distressed situation; the prison having no allowance for firing, nor even bread for the debtors, makes it truly a place of a most melancholy aspect". Many debtors were suffering "excruciating misery", while "many of the other prisoners are nearly naked, having neither linen or scarcely any thing to cover them". Again, the benevolent Oxford public responded, and the following week's newspaper expressed satisfaction that all the prisoners had been able to acquire bread, meat, and fuel as a result of benefactions from six individuals, in addition to half a bushel (the equivalent of four gallons) of coals to each prisoner from a surplus raised in the previous winter. Seven more gifts, totalling £16 (including from Lord and Lady Charles Spencer, Magdalen and Trinity Colleges, and William Jackson, the proprietor of the *Oxford Journal* himself), had been donated for future use.

As the century progressed, occasional attempts were made to enable debtors who met certain conditions to apply for release (such as Thomas Moulden in 1772), but otherwise, a debtor either paid his dues or wasted away from want. Unless you happened to be in residence in late 1786, that is, when something wonderful happened. If debtors often had to rely on help from third parties, so much the better if that third party happened to be the third George! *Jackson's* of 23 September 1786 carried the glad tidings. Following a recent visit to the city, George III had provided £300 to secure the release of as many debtors as were thought deserving. He had also empowered the magistrates to reduce the sentences of any other deserving prisoners. This news, unsurprisingly, was "received by the debtors and prisoners with the most expressive effusions of reverence and gratitude". It was many months before this gratitude was deserved, however, as it was not until April 1787 that the king's benefaction had its effect, enabling 25 of 27 debtors to be freed. Mind you, the Oxford prisoners could perhaps think themselves fortunate that even this long delay was all they had to endure. John Howard, writing in 1789, compared this gift with one of £200 made for identical purposes in Salisbury. Tacitly praising

Daniel Harris, he recorded "with pleasure … this *proper* and *faithful* application of the money" in Oxford, as he was well aware that "part of the donation to Salisbury was spent for the benefit of the gaoler's tap".

Soon after, charity of this kind was not needed at all. During his 1786 visit, George III had also specifically praised "the plan introduced by the magistrates of the county of Oxford of employing the convicts by hard labour within the castle gaol". Not long after, in April 1787, a fund "for establishing pecuniary rewards to be distributed amongst convicts and prisoners" was created. Daniel Harris and William Jackson were among those designated to receive subscriptions, the fund being intended "to give every encouragement to the general plan of reform introduced in the said gaol". The notice requested that "persons visiting the works of the said gaol will not in future give any money to the prisoners or convicts employed there, as they will receive every proper encouragement from the above mentioned institution." No doubt many did, but many others were simply not physically fit enough to respond to that "encouragement" …

Death, disease, and disorder

→>-<←

If Oxford's prisoners were probably luckier than many, the castle was nonetheless a place where hunger, sickness, and untimely death continued on a regular basis, as the insanitary conditions, the poor diet, and the lack of air and exercise took their toll. Outbreaks of gaol fever or distemper were common, as well as the most-feared killer of all – smallpox. John Howard noted that there had been 11 deaths from smallpox in 1773 alone. Several of these occurred in

August and September, entailing a cost for each of five shillings to send a man by horse to fetch the coroner, four shillings for the jury, one shilling and four pence for "bran and wool" (for those unable to afford a coffin), and six shillings to remove the body, the default destination being St Thomas' churchyard. In addition there was the cost of nursing and sustenance, and the coroner's standard charge of £1 plus expenses. Often the coroner gave no precise cause of death, but simply attributed it to the conveniently vague "visitation of God" – a somewhat ironic phrase, in a place which must often have seemed as godforsaken as any.

The year 1775 saw a curious reversal of normal practice, when a Bampton surgeon and apothecary called George Hall placed four notices in *Jackson's* during March, April, and May of that year, inviting the public to visit him *inside* the castle for free consultations. As Hall was imprisoned "through a series of events, as unforeseen and unexpected as unmerited", he requested that the public "will not be prejudiced against him or his medicines on account of his being so unhappy as to be under confinement".* Hall's "unmerited" troubles had begun when he was indicted for conducting smallpox inoculations at the house of an Aston fisherman, William Clarke, on 4 July 1773, whereby "divers filthy and unwholesome smells" were said to have endangered people passing along the adjacent public footpath to Chimney. Both men were fined £20 at the Michaelmas 1773 quarter sessions, but appear to have defaulted, because a further writ was issued at Easter 1774. Undeterred, the defiant Hall wasted no time in announcing in *Jackson's* (30 April 1774) the availability of inoculations at a different house "in the liberties of the hamlets

---

* Hall's earliest notice appeared in *Jackson's* of 22 February 1772, as a surgeon, apothecary, midwife, and bone-setter of Bampton, also selling a medicine of his own creation.

of Aston and Coat", and asked for his previous successes as an apothecary and surgeon to be "an answer to all the abuse which has unjustly (though publickly) been attempted to be thrown upon him by his malicious and self-interested enemy". By implication that enemy was Thomas Horde (probably the grandson of the founder of Horde's Charity – see above), who as Lord of the Manor of Aston had warned the public in *Jackson's* of 17 July 1773 about Hall's "ill nature and insolence" and also about the dangers of wider contagion that his activities posed.

By the summer of 1775, Hall seems to have proved his worth, or improved his abilities, since – now "restored to his liberty" – he advertised his services as a male midwife, operating somewhat brazenly from premises within the same parish of St Peter-le-Bailey within which he had been until very recently a prisoner. Perhaps this was pushing his luck just too far, in a city containing more qualified medical practitioners than most. His last known attempt to seduce the public shows that he had reverted by May 1778 to offering inoculations in a undoubtedly less competitive (and perhaps less regulated) rural location again. This was Appleton, where, he wrote enticingly, "all the beauties of nature that can either please the eye or delight the ear are now in full perfection".

Even with the considerable improvements introduced during Daniel Harris' time as governor, smallpox continued to be a risk. In a letter of 22 June 1790 to the magistrate Christopher Willoughby,* Harris asked for guidance on where he might hold new arrivals, since there had been a recent case among the existing prisoners, which was "an unfortunate circumstance at present as we have so

---

* Willoughby (1749?–1808) chaired the Oxfordshire quarter sessions for more than 20 years. He also, of note, led the committee which raised funds to pay for a memorial to John Howard in St Paul's Cathedral in 1791.

many who have not had it at the gaol". The solution was medical. The following month, according to *Jackson's*, the prisoners were offered inoculations, with the result that "they all experienced the salutary effects which so universally attend this practice".

For some, no amount of surgical assistance could help. Prisons were a repository not just for those intent on criminality or disorder: they held many people too whose only real "crime" was a disorder of the mind. Marshall Tims may have been in this category; William Lardner (probably from the village of Ramsden) certainly was. Dubbed a "madman" in the quarter sessions documentation, he slit his own throat on 21 January 1721, yet still it required three people to watch over him until he died five days later – a necessary precaution, probably, as Lardner's violent nature is evidenced by a bill for five shillings for "damage done to a bed … breaking down the bedstead". Another, posthumous, cost of five shillings was for "a woman for washing the bed and bedding which he had bled on".

The Black Assize of 6 July 1577

+>-<+

Death, then, has been no stranger to Oxford Castle, but never more than in July 1577, as a result of Oxford's infamous "Black Assize". Accounts of this strange episode vary, but probably the most reliable is that in Anthony Wood's *History and Antiquities of the University of Oxford* (1684), his main source being the register of Merton College. The man at the centre of the incident was a bookbinder called Rowland Jencks, a Roman Catholic of Belgian extraction, who "would not only rail against the Commonwealth, but the Religion now established, and by the generality in the University embraced". Eventually, the authorities felt obliged to act. He was arrested in May 1577 and stood trial at the following assizes, held then (but never again) in the old Shire Hall within the castle complex (see Figures 2, 3, and 4). When the verdict was delivered on 6 July, the "saucy and foul-mouthed" Jencks heard that he was to lose his ears. No sooner had this bizarre punishment been pronounced by the judge than "there arose such an infectious damp or breath among the people, that many there present ... were then smothered, and others so deeply infected that they lived not many hours after".

Six hundred people sickened in Oxford that same day, plus a further 100 who had returned to their homes in outlying villages. Wood described the ensuing weeks for the victims as "very calamitous and full of sorrow, occasioned by the rage of their disease and pain" which caused them to "beat their keepers or nurses, and drive them from their presence. Others like mad men would run about the streets, markets and lanes, and other places. Some again would leap headlong into deep waters."

On 12 August, the contagion ceased as suddenly as it had begun, the death toll having reached 300 in Oxford and 210 elsewhere. The victims included most of the magistrates who had presided at the assize, including the sheriff, Sir Robert d'Oyley (a relative, though not direct descendant, of the first Norman custodian of the castle), nearly all the jury, and 100 scholars. Yet the fatal malady affected no women or children, nor anyone who was poor, nor indeed Jencks himself, leading almost inevitably to a conclusion of either divine influence or sorcery – although the true cause was almost certainly an extreme case of gaol fever (or typhus), a virulent infection spawned by the "nasty and pestilential smell of the prisoners" in the heat of summer. At the time, prisoners were brought to the Shire Hall along an underground passageway which led directly from their cells, so transmission was quite feasible, the prisoners themselves having probably built up some kind of immunity. Certainly Jencks himself survived, and emigrated to the pro-Catholic environs of the French town of Douai. There he lived to an old age – until at least 1610, according to Wood – although the tumultuous events of the Black Assize did not spare him his sentence, and he did so minus his ears!

Were the lessons of the Black Assize learned? Not according to John Howard, who when visiting in 1780 felt it probable that

> the rooms in this castle are the same as the prisoners occupied at the time of the *Black Assize*. The wards are close and offensive, so that if crowded, I should not greatly wonder to hear of another *fatal assize* at Oxford.

It was an opinion that Edward (alias John) Lambo(u)rn of Nettlebed, John Higden of Wallingford, Mathew Pebworth of Witney, Mathew Smith of Oxford, and David Brod(e)rick of Islip might have shared earlier in the century. All had been sentenced to transportation, and their petition of Michaelmas 1720 advised that they were "in great want and have not sufficient allowance to keep us alive nor nothing to cover our nakedness nor nothing to ley upon butt the bare boards". Rather than endure this situation any longer, their desperation was such that they begged to be "carried to the place which we are cast for or else take us all out and hange us out of such a lingering life". The latter drastic remedy proved unnecessary as all five men were transported the following year, but for many others, hanging did indeed mark the termination of their time at Oxford Castle. The following chapters recount a few of the most remarkable.

CHAPTER SIX

EXECUTIONS (1)
"The Unfathomable Gulf of Eternity"

The preceding chapters introduced a few of the men and women who made a living from their positions of authority within Oxford Castle, and some of the more interesting and unfortunate prisoners for whom they were responsible. Those who escaped mostly found their freedom short-lived. Those transported to the colonies exchanged one form of confinement for another, but, however uncertain and gruelling their prospects, they were at least facing a future with a defined end. Capital convicts too were in no doubt about their fates, once any chance of a reprieve had passed, and many seem to have found a morbid solace in this inevitability, as preferable to months or even years of uncertainty.

The final chapters of this book describe the circumstances which resulted in some of Oxford's most remarkable public hangings to the end of Daniel Harris' period as governor of the prison in 1809. The location was always in one of two places: either Green Ditch (also known as "Gallows Baulk"), on the Banbury Road, exactly one mile from the city's central point of Carfax, or within the castle precincts. Green Ditch was where residents of the city tended to be executed, until at least 1757, which is the last occasion specifically identified by *Jackson's Oxford Journal* (see Appendix 3). The castle was usually where prisoners who were from elsewhere in the county, or who were from other parts of the country but had committed their crimes in Oxfordshire, met their ends. Much of the information in this chapter comes from *Jackson's*, which seems faithfully to have reported every execution after its launch in 1753. Before that, the absence of records means that a very large number of executions will probably never be revealed.* Hangings deemed of sufficient interest were often described in broadsides or longer contemporary pamphlets (many are at the Oxfordshire Record Office and Bodleian Library), but often the location itself is not specified. After 1757 it is likely that all executions took place at the castle; from 1787 onwards they certainly did. That year saw the first hanging above the new main gateway facing New Road, which provided an elevated platform from where the gallows could be displayed to maximum effect. The other advantage of this arrangement was that it saw the end of the riotous scenes which had so often accompanied ground-level executions, after which the servants of the University's anatomists engaged with the relatives or friends of the deceased in undignified and often violent struggles for possession of the body. Additional tensions were created by the widely held belief that it was efficacious to touch the body of a hanged man, or his clothes, or the rope.†

However, this elevated prominence presented some condemned men with an opportunity to enhance their fame through the delivery of a "gallows speech" of varying degrees of remorse or defiance. The judicial logic had been that because only a relatively small number

---

* Appendix 1 presents the most complete list ever published.
† Thomas Hardy's *The Withered Arm* (set in 1825) explores this theme.

of criminals were ever actually apprehended, it was important to make an example of those who were. Yet as more and more people used their last moments to increase their notoriety rather than admit their guilt, to sow doubts in the public mind, rather than acquiesce in a humiliating public death, the efficacy of public executions as a display of the grand omnipotence of the law began to be questioned – although it took a very long time, until 1863, in fact, for the spectacle ultimately to be abolished in Oxford (see Appendix 1).

Most executions were, unsurprisingly, of men, but there was a particular gender-specific crime which resulted in more executions of women than would otherwise have been the case. This was infanticide, the murder of a (usually illegitimate) newborn infant. This crime was an exception in English law to the usual "innocent-unless-proven-guilty" status of any accused person, since if the mother was unmarried guilt was assumed unless at least one witness could be summoned to assert that there had been a stillbirth. Almost inevitably an unmarried mother would not want anyone to know of her pregnancy, hence the reason why so many were found guilty, and why at least half of all recorded cases of female execution at Oxford were for this reason.

The earliest documented Oxfordshire case concerned a poor, unexceptional individual, but one whose fame has outlasted most others because of her ability to cheat the hangman's noose and almost literally rise again from the grave. At least three contemporary pamphlets were published, the most reliable probably being *Newes from the Dead*, the author, Richard Watkins, a sometime student at Christ Church, having gleaned his information "from those that were the chiefe Instruments bringing this great work to perfection". It is this account from which most of the quotations which follow are taken.

"Newes from the Dead":
Anne Green

-+>-<+-

Anne Green was hanged at the castle on Saturday 14 December 1650 for the murder of her newborn child. Born at Steeple Barton in about 1628, she was a servant at the house of Sir Thomas Read at Duns Tew, and was described as being "of a middle stature, strong, fleshie, and of an indifferent good feature". In an age-old scenario, she attracted the unscrupulous attentions of a male member of her employer's household, Jeffrey Read, the adolescent grandson of Sir Thomas, by whom she was "often solicited by fair promises and

FIGURE 19 The woodcut accompanying *Newes from the Dead* (1651). Note the man pulling down on Anne Green's legs to try to hasten her death and the soldier striking her with his musket, to ascertain if she had expired.

other amorous enticements". She managed to hide the ensuing pregnancy, attending to her duties as normal until November 1650, when, as she was working in Read's malt house

> a child about a span long sprung from her, but abortive, which much improved her health and strength, but being exceeding fearful that a discovery should be made thereof, she laid it in a corner of the aforesaid house and covered it with dust and rubbish.

When another servant informed Sir Thomas, he made immediate arrangements for Anne to be sent to Oxford Castle, presumably intending to suppress any scandal by procuring a swift verdict. There she spent the next three weeks "in continual affrights and terrors, in a place as comfortless as her condition", until her case was heard at a specially convened assize, overseen (according to Dr Robert Plot, in *Natural History of Oxfordshire*, 1677) by Sergeant Umpton Croke of Marston. Despite the strong likelihood of stillbirth, she was almost inevitably found guilty of infanticide and sentenced to hang.

At the execution, held early in the morning within the castle grounds, Anne Green exhibited "an undauntedness of spirit" and "at the going up the ladder, she fixt her eyes on the executioner, saying, God forgive my false accusers, as I freely forgive thee". In a short address to the crowd, she said that her impending death "doth not in the least strike dread and terror to my heart, but rather incites me to a notion of eternal joy and happiness, for I conceive there is no more than this rope and ladder between me and Heaven". She remained hanging for half an hour. This was more than a century before the introduction of the "drop" (first used at Tyburn in 1759 and universally in 1783), when death would be instantaneous as the victim's neck was broken as a result of the sudden fall. Before then, hanging meant slow asphyxiation, and it was common practice to ask friends and relatives to try to expedite the process. Consequently,

> some of her friends in the meantime thumping her on the breast, others hanging with all their weight upon her legges, sometimes lifting her up, and then pulling her downe again with a suddaine jerke, thereby the sooner to dispatch her out of her paine: insomuch as the under-sheriffe fearing lest thereby they should break the rope, forbad them to do so any longer.

In addition: "A soldier standing by gave her 4 or 5 blowes on the brest, with the but end of his musket." It having thus been established that the young woman had truly expired, her body was taken to the house of an apothecary called Clark, ready for dissection. Before any medical men had arrived, however, some lingering signs of life were detected, so

> a lusty fellow that stood by (thinking to do an act of charity in ridding her out of the small reliques of a painful life) stamped several times on her breast and stomach with all the force he could.

Plot named this man as Mason, a tailor, and added that a soldier, whom he identified as Orum, struck her again with the butt end of his musket. Yet despite all, Anne Green refused to die. Two doctors, William Petty and Thomas Willis (of Christ Church), arrived at about 9am and, on detecting signs of life, attempted various treatments to revive her.* This included the standard measure of bleeding. Still insensible, she was left to sleep, and a woman was paid to lie next to her to keep her warm.

---

* Petty (1623–1687) was a fellow of Brasenose College, and, his reputation hugely enhanced through the Green case, became in 1662 an original member of the Royal Society. Willis (1621–1675) is described in the *Dictionary of National Biography* as "a leader among the Oxford virtuosi in both chemistry and anatomy".

The next day, Sunday, Petty and Willis returned with some other doctors at 8am, to find Green recovered and talking, her first words having been, "Behold God's providence, and His wonder of wonders". Though obviously still in pain, an hour later "she laughed and talked merrily, looking fresh and of a good colour". On the Monday the doctors questioned her in private about her recollections. She answered "that after she put off some of her clothes, bequeathing them to her mother (which was early in the morning, before her execution) and heard someone say that one of the prisoners was let out of the chaine to put her to death, she remembered nothing at all". This was not the exclusive glimpse of the afterlife that the Oxford academics had been hoping for; but despite all entreaties, Anne Green was never able to recollect what had happened after her fetters had been removed, save for a vague recollection of "a fellow wrapt up in a blanket, which indeed was the habit of the executioner".

As news spread of this minor miracle, an armed guard was needed to keep away the inquisitive crowds. Anne's father (whom Petty names as William) opportunistically stationed himself at the house, in order to accept donations from "those of the better sort" who wished to get a glimpse of his daughter, who had changed, almost literally overnight, from a cause of disgrace for the family to one of great value. These funds paid for the apothecary's bill, her food and lodging, and part of the cost of her eventual pardon. By 19 December, five days after the hanging, she had recovered sufficiently to walk with assistance, and to eat her first substantial food, and eight to ten days later she went to stay with friends in her home village of Steeple Barton, "taking away with her the coffin wherein she lay as a trophey of this, her wonderful preservation".

Annexed to Richard Watkin's *Newes from the Dead* were numerous poems and ballads (including one by Anthony Wood). That by John

Mainard of Magdalen College demonstrates some clever wordplay while taking the opportunity to highlight the culpability of the Read family:

> Sure death abhorres the colour, all have seene
> That Death is blacke, and therefore loves no *Green*!
> A happy colour, in what Praedicament
> Will the Logicians put this Accident?
> Shee had her Neck-verse; 'tis a currant signe
> Shee could not read, her verse was but a Line.*
>
> Againe, upon this deed to set a crowne;
> Sh'ad been cut up, if not so soon cut downe.
> Read this thou youthfull *Read*, and be afraid.
> Shee's a maid twice, and yet is not *dis-maid*.
> O Paradoxe! If truth in thee can lye,
> No wonder if the maid could live and dye.

The contribution of Edward Norreys (a student of Queen's College from Weston-on-the-Green) is addressed directly to her would-be executioner:

> To the Hangman:
> Come *Flesh-Crow*, tell me, what's the Cause that you
> Rigour to Men, to Women favour show?
> Your Office you have not performed, 'tis plaine:
> See, here's the Wench you hang'd, alive againe.
> Yet, for this once, I'le cleare you; it was not
> Your *slack rope* sav'd her, nor your *fast-loose* knot.
> Her fatall halter shee (to end the strife)
> Untwisted spun into a thread of life.

---

* An apparent reference to "Benefit of the Clergy".

In a final poignant twist, the "thread of life" of her persecutor, Sir Thomas Read, lasted only a few days after Anne Green's recovery. His burial at Duns Tew on 20 December 1650 occurred just as his former servant was starting to regain her own vitality. Many no doubt saw this as a sign of divine justice. Anne Green's "resurrection" was certainly seen in this light: she was pardoned of her supposed crime, and, it is pleasing to note, was able to go on to lead an apparently conventional life in the neighbouring parish of Westcote Barton, after marrying John Taylor on 29 May 1651 at Tadmarton. No doubt adding to the Read family's embarrassment, Taylor was from Duns Tew. The couple had three sons baptised between April 1652 and July 1656, but Anne Green's own life came to an end in 1662. Although she was still of a relatively young age, she must have felt that that extra decade was a bonus indeed.* The story of another woman whose circumstances eight years later were very similar had a much less happy ending, however.

"A poor maid from Magdalen parish": Elizabeth Russell

-+->-<-+-

Anthony Wood is the original source for the story of a second botched execution of another young woman accused of causing the death of her newborn illegitimate child. He recorded the hanging at Green Ditch on Tuesday 4 May 1658 in *Life and Times,* and Robert Plot (1677) later identified her as Elizabeth, the servant of Mrs Cope of Magdalen parish. He wrote that she

---

* Anne Green's story was fictionalised by Mary Hooper in 2008, under the same historical title of *Newes from the Dead.*

hung for so long that one of the by-standers scrupled not to say that if she were not dead he would be hanged for her: hereupon being cut down (the gallows being very high) she fell with such violence on the ground that it would have been enough to have been the death of many another person, only to have had such a fall.

Her body was taken away to be dissected, but, just as with the resilient Anne Green, she revived, and was taken instead to the George Inn in Magdalen parish (according to Plot), where a St John's College physician, Dr William Coniers, attended her. Also like Green, she underwent bleeding, and another woman lay next to her to keep her warm.

So far so good. But when the city bailiffs heard what had happened, they too made their way to the George, arriving soon after midnight, intent on finishing the job. Still in her coffin, Elizabeth was conveyed to Broken Hayes (now Gloucester Green), where the bailiffs "put a halter about her neck and plucked her out of a coffin over one of the trees there". This time there was no mistake, but local people were so enraged that according to Wood the tree in question was felled afterwards in protest. Neither Wood nor Plot reveal the fate of her corpse, but it seems safe to assume that with local resentment running so high no further attempt was made to claim the body for dissection, and that she was Elizabeth Russell, whose burial at St Mary Magdalen took place on 5 May. Henry Mallory, the chief bailiff, was vilified thereafter, to the extent that he was forced to cease trading as a cutler, the general opinion being that his subsequent impoverishment was because "God's judgements followed him for the cruelty he shew'd to the poore maid".

Two more cases of infanticide:
"good people, all pray for me"

→>-<←

The public executions of only 12 women can be discerned in Oxford between 1650 and 1766 (see Appendix 1). Of these, at least six were for infanticide. There were doubtless many more such early cases, the records of which have not survived, but by the 1760s we have *Jackson's Oxford Journal* on which to rely. On 31 July 1762 Susan Harris, a servant to a Sydenham farmer called Taylor, was hanged at Oxford Castle. Harris had delivered herself of a baby girl at around 3am one morning, and when Taylor's wife, who had long suspected her of being pregnant, went up to her room at 5am, "the child was found in a cupboard in her bed-chamber wrapped up in a sheet". Also executed the same day was James Costard of Benson. He had been found guilty of the murder of his mother, who expired instantly when he fired a pistol "so close to her as to set her cap and handkerchief on fire". Harris behaved "very decently" at the execution, according to *Jackson's*, which quotes her last words as: "Father pray for me, Mother pray for me, good people, all pray for me". Then came a clue as to how Anne Green and the maid known only as Elizabeth might have survived their ordeals: "Before the cart drew away, she sank down and thereby the knot slipping to her chin, the noose did not draw, and they were obliged to raise a ladder, and lift up the body, till the cord was better fixed."

The last public hanging of any woman in Oxford occurred on 10 March 1766, and yet again the crime for which she suffered was infanticide. But it was an incident with a twist, because it was not the mother of the newborn child who was found guilty, but its grandmother. Mary Lampry or Lamphrey and her daughter Ann had been at work in the fields near their Kingham home in the previous August.* When the sound of an infant's cries attracted the attention of some other labourers, the two women attempted to behave as if nothing was wrong, but the tiny body was found "dead upon the ground under one of them, wrapped up in a piece of flannel". The conclusion was that "it had not only been strangled with a cord but that its body was also crushed flat by having been set or laid upon". Mary Lampry was sent immediately to the castle; her daughter followed a month later, when she had recovered her strength. Both were condemned to death at the following March assizes, but only the older woman suffered that fate, confessing only a few minutes before her execution that "she was the sole cause of the child's death, and that her daughter was perfectly innocent, and in a swoon during the whole of that transaction". Ann was consequently granted an initial respite of ten days, and ultimately given a free pardon.

"Gentlemen, do not hang me high": Mary Blandy of Henley

➤➤◄◄

There was no such reprieve for Mary Blandy (c.1719–1752), Oxfordshire's most famous eighteenth-century murderess, though she continued to protest her innocence and hope for clemency right to the end. Blandy was an exception to the general rule of a person from an impoverished background drawn by design or circumstance into a life of crime – or indeed into committing just a single crime

---

* William Lampry married Mary Greyhurst of Kingham at Chipping Norton on 30 January 1732. Their daughter Ann was baptised at Kingham on 5 June 1738. William was buried in 1755. To compound the tragedy of the Lampry family, he had hanged himself.

– as a means of improving a miserable or downtrodden existence. For she was the daughter of a well-known Henley attorney, Francis Blandy, and it was her own father who was the victim. In a way he was the author of his own misfortune. When his wife died in October 1749, Francis decided that it was high time that his only child, soon to turn 30, should wed. This should not have posed any particular difficulty, since even in one of the more unsympathetic contemporary publications about her case she was described as "of middle size, well-shaped, of a brown complexion, with black eyes, full of fire, and tho' not a beauty, is very agreeable, especially when she speaks, and her conversation is full of wit and good sense". Yet Francis had a reputation as a somewhat pompous man, fond of emphasising his eminent connections, and he contrived to improve Mary's marriage prospects by exaggerating the extent of his wealth, and therefore of her future inheritance.

The ploy worked – but with fatal consequences. An impoverished army captain called William Henry Cranstoun (1714–1752), who had first met her in 1746 while visiting his uncle Sir Mark Ker at his Henley residence of Paradise House, became suddenly enamoured of Mary after a gap of years. The feelings were reciprocated, but a soldier, however well connected – Cranstoun was a younger son of a minor Scottish nobleman – was not at all the sort of match that Francis had in mind, so he forbade any further contact. Cranstoun was consistently identified as considerably older than her in contemporary accounts, though in truth was only a few years her senior, looking, it would seem, rather older than his true age: "diminutive in stature, disfigured by the small pox, so as to have his face all in seams, blear-eyed, and of a very mean aspect". Despite this, he had some indefinable attraction for the opposite sex. Indeed, as it later turned out, he already had a wife and child in Scotland,

and was also rumoured to have fathered an illegitimate child in London. Mary was nonetheless smitten, and the pair contrived to remove the barrier to their love, namely her father. Cranstoun, back in Scotland, sent Mary some arsenic powder, which she then administered in her father's food. At least, that was the reality; at her trial she averred, somewhat implausibly, that Cranstoun had assured her that the powder was merely a kind of "love potion" which would make her father better disposed towards him and his matrimonial intentions. Whatever, Mary proved an incompetent would-be patricide, and before her father finally succumbed on Wednesday 14 August 1751, the family's washerwoman and chambermaid had both been made seriously unwell as a result of consuming the tainted remains of Francis' unfinished food.

Despite all the evidence, the Henley authorities were reluctant to accept that a likeable young woman from their own social elite could commit such a deed. The townspeople were less sceptical, however, and when Mary appeared to be attempting to leave town the following morning, exactly as the autopsy was being conducted, they took it upon themselves to prevent her. As a result, she got no further than the Angel Inn, on the Berkshire side of the Thames, while the mob lurked outside. It was a situation which gave the still slightly apologetic Henley authorities the pretext they needed – to detain her for her own safety. When arsenic was detected in the dead man's stomach, an inevitable conclusion was drawn, and Mary was taken immediately to Oxford Castle, being therefore poignantly absent from her own father's funeral on 17 August.

Obliged to wait until the next assizes, for Mary Blandy her stay in the castle was by no means as unpleasant as for many. A woman of her standing was allowed her own room in the prison (seemingly within the house provided for the gaoler William Wisdom), to have

FIGURE 20 An image from *A Genuine Account of the most Horrid Parricide committed by Mary Blandy*. It was printed by C. Goddard of Oxford (for sale by William Jackson's former newspaper partner, Robert Walker in London) in 1751, long before her trial, the title being, therefore, somewhat presumptuous! The scene shows her taking tea with a friend, Mrs Dean, to all appearances as if she were entertaining at her home in Henley. Only the small fetters around her ankles show that all is not as it seems.

a former maid, Mrs Dean, in attendance, and to entertain visitors. As an account published before the trial stated, she was "serene and calm … always drinking tea twice a day, sometimes walking in the keeper's garden with a guard, and playing at cards in the evening".

Several pamphlets, most of them condemnatory, were published before and after her trial (which was on 3 March 1752) and execution (a month later). One (*A genuine and impartial account of the life of Miss Mary Blandy*, sold by William Jackson, from where most of the quotations below derive) revealed that a false rumour about the day of her execution had resulted in a crowd gathering prematurely at the Castle Green. Blandy

> went up several times into the rooms facing the green, where she could view the great crowd of people about it, which she did with all the calmness and unconcern imaginable, and only said she would not balk their expectations, tho' her execution might be deferred a day or two longer.

It was, until the following Monday, April 6th. At 10pm on the Sunday, hearing that the sheriff was in town, a necessary precursor to any execution, Blandy requested that she should not be disturbed before 8am. During the night she arose at 4am and went upstairs to contemplate the gallows, which were "opposite the door of the gaol, and made by laying a pole across upon the arms of two trees".* At half past eight she spent 30 minutes in prayer with the prison chaplain, the Rev. Swinton, and was then led outside, holding two guineas in her hand for the executioner.

---

* The word "tree" was often employed to mean "gallows" and implies the upright posts or gibbet, not a living tree. It was common practice for the condemned person, from royalty downwards, to provide remuneration to the executioner, in order to encourage a swift and efficient job.

Blandy was a member of the establishment, for whom appearances counted – even at the very last moment. Her attire was therefore carefully chosen, and equally carefully described in all the accounts, as a black Bombazine short sack (a loose-fitting gown) and petticoat, with a clean white handkerchief drawn over her face. Her hands were tied with a strong black ribbon – a Paduasoy ribbon, in fact, as one writer found it necessary to specify!

Before ascending the ladder, Blandy made the expected and customary speech, and, still maintaining her innocence, "behaved with such serenity and composure, and with such a decent resolution, as greatly surprised and charmed many of the spectators". Depending which account you choose to believe, those spectators numbered either 5,000 or very few. Either way, it was noted that "contrary to what is observed at other executions, there was almost profound silence" as many of those present were moved to tears.

On the fifth step of the ladder, she uttered some words which had a particular significance for any female, conscious of the likely prurient attention of a predominantly male crowd: "Gentlemen, do not hang me high for the sake of decency," she requested, before ascending two more steps. Then the halter was put about her neck, her eyes were covered, and the ladder was turned. In accordance with her request, her feet almost touched the ground, so her modesty was preserved – at least for the half-hour that her body remained suspended. But no-one seems to have thought to provide a coffin. Perhaps the confusion about the day of execution had deterred those who might otherwise have made the journey from Henley; perhaps there was an expectation that somehow an otherwise blameless woman of her rank would, in the end, somehow manage to acquire a reprieve; or perhaps her acquaintances were resigned to the effect of a new statute that required the bodies of all murderers to be delivered by law for anatomisation (see Appendix 4). Whatever, with no coffin available, her body "was carried through the crowd upon the shoulders of one of the sheriff's men in the most beastly manner, with her legs exposed very indecently for several hundred yards, and then deposited in the sheriff's man's house". A hearse was found, however, and departed at 5.30pm for Henley. The fact that her father had, in his last moments, forgiven her, is perhaps why it was decided to permit her body to be interred that same night in the chancel of the church, next to both her mother and, with decided poignancy, the father of whose death she had been the cause.*

One might expect that the scarcity of historical Oxfordshire murders by females would be counterbalanced by a very much larger number of men. Surprisingly perhaps, that is not the case (see Appendix 1). What is less surprising, because it reflects a well-known general trait, is that of the 16 known Oxfordshire murders by men between 1650 and 1800, almost all concerned victims with whom they were already intimate. Two of the earliest for which there are detailed accounts both concerned the murder of wives by their husbands.

---

* The register of St Mary's, Henley-on-Thames, records Francis Blandy's burial on 17 August 1751, with the added comment: "Attorney at Law was poysoned by his only child Mary Blandy". Mary Blandy's entry for 6 April 1752 has also been annotated to the effect that she had "poysoned" her father. Cranstoun had fled the country, and, to round off a tragic tale of futile greed, vanity, and deceit, he died of illness in Flanders before the end of that same year of 1752. A splendidly vivid and convincing fictionalised version of the story is told in *Mary Blandy* by Joan Morgan (1979), first published as *The Hanging Wood* in 1950.

"As innocent … as the child that is unborn": John Protheroe of Barton

→>-<-

John Protheroe was executed on Monday 22 March 1725 for the murder of his pregnant wife, a jury having decided that after ten years of marriage he had found "his wife's love in a declining condition towards him and his family", as it was phrased in a broadside of the case. The prelude to this fateful moment was that over the years his wife had been spending more and more time in the ale-house next door to their home in Barton. The Oxford diarist Thomas Hearne retained a copy of this broadside in his diary (now in the Bodleian Library), and added the names of Mary Bailey and Sampson Bowles as the people who, over a period of 18 months, were supposed to have "oftentimes by perswasion and once by force attempted to debauch" Protheroe's wife (whose first name is never mentioned). However, it was believed that they had become reconciled, and on the night in question had gone to bed as usual. A few hours later his wife "awaken'd him, and desired him to arise and help the children to make water as usual, after which time she desired him to fetch her some beer, saying she was very ill". So ill indeed that by the time Protheroe returned he found her "struggling as it were for life". It was a struggle that she lost, the subsequent efforts of Protheroe and their neighbour Mary Bailey to revive her proving ineffectual. This being the case, the broadside maintained, Protheroe was "as innocent … as the child that is unborn".

However, Hearne denounced the piece as a "downright formal lye", saying that the 33-year-old Protheroe "had been a sad, vile wretch and is said to have murdered one of his children before. Not one person appeared in his behalf, no not even at his execution, even so much as to take care of his corps". Whatever the actual rights and wrongs of the case, Hearne's denunciation of this particular broadside reflects the caution needed in assessing the veracity of all such publications.

"'Twas made a skeleton and the flesh dispersed up and down": William Fuller of Caversham

→>-<-

A few years later, a similar case of the murder of a spouse is interesting not so much for the actual crime, but for the extraordinary violence which followed the resultant execution. It is again Thomas Hearne whom we have to thank for some of the details. On 30 July 1730 he noted that after the hanging two days earlier of William Fuller, 26, from Caversham, a dispute arose over possession of the body.* Some scholars attempted to secure it for anatomisation, but when others in the crowd resisted, a mêlée broke out and the coffin that had been provided by Fuller's relatives was smashed to bits, with the corpse still inside it, "and so for several times sometimes one side had it and sometimes the other". When some University proctors arrived, the scholars desisted, and another coffin was hastily contrived. Soon after, however, the scholars then

> rescued the body, cutt off the head etc.; after which 'twas again recovered for the relations, and then got from them again and brought to Queen's College, where 'twas made a skeleton and the flesh dispersed up and down.

---

* Although Hearne actually wrote "Richard", the newspaper accounts all state "William", a possible candidate being William, the son of Thomas and Hester Fuller, baptised in Abingdon on 15 December 1705.

Inside Hearne's original diary there is a cutting from *Northampton Mercury* of 5 August, which provided a slightly different, slightly less gruesome account. Here it was said that during the "desperate riot" the body was carried initially to Lincoln College, but then rescued from there by the University proctors, who secreted it in a house in Bullock's [i.e. Bulwarks] Lane. Undeterred, the scholars "went and broke open the doors and carryed it off" again, only for the proctors to retrieve it once more. Subsequently: "The tumult was so extraordinary that the town-clerk was forced to read the proclamation, but to no purpose, the rioter crying out they did not hear it." This time the proctors took Fuller's corpse to the far more secure environs of the castle, so, in an ironic twist, the place which had kept him safely away from the public while he was alive was keeping the public away from him now he was dead! At 11pm, "when all was thought still", his corpse was moved "to the water-side to send it away in a boat". However, this was still not the end of the gruesome episode: "to their surprize, the scholars were lying in ambush". In desperation Fuller's friends threw his corpse into the water, "coffin and all, but the scholars soon went in, in great numbers, and drew it out and carried it to Christ's College to dissect it".*

Hearne does not specify from which colleges these determined scholars came, but this 1733 comment from *Speech as it was Spoken at the Public Act* by "Terrae Filius" (a kind of Georgian Oxford University *Private Eye*) points to Jesus College: "Methinks, I scent toasted Cheese, sure we are upon the Welsh Borders. See the Fabrick founded by Queen Elizabeth for the Jolly Cambro-Britons ... Here

---

* A third account, in two London newspapers, placed this incident earlier in the day, noting that once the coffin had been projected into the stream (presumably the Trill Mill Stream), "the gownsmen then jump'd in like spaniels" to retrieve it.

are your heroes that vanquish Bargemen and carry off the dead Bodies in triumph to be anatomiz'd." The scholars of Jesus College (founded exclusively for men of Welsh origin) had a reputation for frequent and effective participation in Oxford's regular Town and Gown riots; bargemen enjoyed a similar pugilistic renown, and for that reason their services were often solicited by friends or relatives of the deceased.

A prime example of this was at the execution of two highwaymen, Acton Brice and Richard Bayliss, on 22 March 1754. Afterwards, some 50 bargemen "armed with clubs, hangers, knives &c. ... carried away the bodies in triumph", in defiance of the University (*Public Advertiser* 25 March 1754). A year later a dispute arose over rights to the body of an executed sheep-thief called Robert Randall. It "occasioned a pitch'd battle" between a "celebrated champion" and former horse-taker called James Carter and a bargeman called William Briscoe. They settled their differences at the Holywell Cockpit the same afternoon, when "Carter shewed himself thoroughly *game* by giving out thoroughly satisfied in about three minutes" (*Jackson's,* 3 May 1755).

A "diabolical instance of barbarity": Robert Hitchcock of Combe

→►◄←

One other example of the murder of a close relative deserves mention, as a rare example of the condemned man being completely content to allow his corpse to be dissected. Robert Hitchcock was a wealthy farmer from Combe, near Woodstock, and was executed on Monday 9 March 1778 for what was described uncompromisingly in a broadside as "the most diabolical instance of barbarity ever remembered in a civilised nation". This was the murder of his 81-year-old father, Edward, in the previous July. Hitchcock, an only son, had hardly been subtle about his "barbarity". At the trial 13 witnesses swore that "in the course of a few hours they saw the prisoner beat, bruise, and kick his aged parent upon the road in his way from Bloxham to Coombe in a most shocking and inhuman manner". The fact that none of them thought it necessary to intervene was considered almost equally shocking: "it is almost wonderful … that there should be no man so far impelled by the feelings of humanity as to rescue a miserable being from the hands of his murderer". To be fair, some sympathetic individuals had stepped in earlier to thwart Hitchcock's plan to abandon his father in the Banbury parish in which he had been born,* but after that the old man was at his son's mercy. It took the two of them until 3am to complete their 14-mile journey back to Combe that day, and Edward was found dead the following morning.

During the four-hour trial, Hitchcock remained unrepentant, even when it was revealed that this was not an isolated instance of brutality towards his father, the broadside noting that he had often "forced him to undergo labour beyond his strength, and after cruelly beating and whipping the old man, whilst fainting under the fatigue, frequently to have tied him to the harness of his horses and let the team drag him along". Hitchcock's only response was that his actions were justified because his father was "frequently insane and subject to fits". Unsurprisingly, it was a defence which failed!†

---

* This would appear to have been Horton (near Banbury), where Robert, the son of Edward and Lucy "Hitchcox" was baptised on 25 December 1737. Edward's burial was at Combe on 20 July 1777.
† A detailed transcript of the trial was published by William Jackson in 1778 as *Trial at Large of Robert Hitchcock*.

On the day of the execution, Hitchcock showed greater penitence. Poignantly dressed in the same clothes that he had worn at his father's funeral, he spent 15 minutes in prayer beneath the gallows, and specifically requested that his body might be delivered for dissection "without molestation". He need not have worried: the undignified scenes which marked the conclusion of many earlier executions did not occur, as no sympathisers were present, and the agents of Christ Church Anatomy School were able to claim their prize without incident. Another beneficiary was Mrs Hitchcock, who remarried the very next month, considerably the richer for having inherited her dead husband's sizeable fortune.

"Cut off from the face of the earth": George Strap of Bicester

-+->-<+-

Almost all the cases so far recounted in this chapter have concerned the murder of a relative of the perpetrator. One exception, and one where the accused was as careless a contributor to his discovery as any, concerned George Strap, who was executed on Monday 13 March 1775 for the murder of his employer, Edward Bowden, a cobbler of Bicester.* When Bowden failed to open his shop one morning, the alarm was raised. Strap, effecting gallantry, offered to ascend a ladder in order to investigate, but, somewhat tellingly, "it was observed that before he was high enough to see into the room, he told the people assembled that his master had not been in bed". Bowden's neighbours then decided to break in to ascertain the truth. There they found Bowden's lifeless body. He had been

* Edward Bowden was buried at Bicester on 24 November 1774.

hit on the head, and his throat had been slit "quite round so as to almost sever his head from his body". With suspicions already aroused, Strap made his second mistake later that day, by allowing himself to be surprised in the act of trying to wash blood from his clothes – a man caught almost literally red-handed, then, in the accepted origin of the phrase. The motive was afterwards assumed to have been greed: Bowden was known to have told Strap that he had 15 guineas on the premises.

At the trial, Strap persisted in pleading his innocence at first, but ultimately acknowledged his guilt. The long eloquent verdict delivered by Justice Nares concluded with the phrase that "you are to be cut off from the face of the earth", to which, according to a broadside, Strap responded, "I say so too". The execution was witnessed by the diarist James Woodforde, by then a sub-warden and pro-proctor of New College:

> He confessed (just as he came out of the castle) the crime for which he suffered, but not before. He pulled up his cap two or three times to delay. A Methodist prayed by him in the cart some time under the gallows. He seemed full hardy. It is said that he declared yesterday, if he had only his liberty for one quarter of an hour, he would employ it in murdering of his wife. I think I never saw such sullenness & villainy on one face. Jack Ketch kissed him twice before he went off.* His body was carried to Dr. Parsons's,† to be dissected and anatomized pursuant to the Sentence. I do believe that there were more than six thousand spectators present when he was hanged.

* Jack Ketch was England's most famous seventeenth-century executioner. His name was adopted as a generic for anyone undertaking this role until well into the twentieth century (see Appendix 3).
† John Parsons was the first Lee Reader in Anatomy at Christ Church.

"Such odious detestation that ... not a tear of pity was extorted": Edward Thorn of Henley

-+->-<-+-

The final case of murder within the period covered by this book concerned probably the oldest person executed at Oxford, Edward Thorn. Thorn was baptised at Steventon on 30 November 1740, and died on Monday 28 July 1800.* Thorn was the landlord of the White Hart at Northfield End, Henley. In the previous March, the body of Amy Jacob, one of his staff, was discovered there. Suspicions were aroused when Thorn absconded before the jury assembled for the inquest had reached a decision, which was that she had been poisoned. Another pertinent fact was revealed too: that she was pregnant. Thorn was captured within days, and his case was hardly helped at the subsequent trial by the damning evidence of a Henley apothecary, who testified that Thorn had earlier asked him for advice on how to terminate a pregnancy. A few days later, Thorn had purchased some ratsbane, the same poison as was discovered in the girl's stomach. At the trial, the judge underlined that even if Thorn had merely intended to give Amy Jacob "the fatal drug ... to cause abortion, it was equally criminal in the eye of the law as if given to destroy the life of the girl". This chapter has portrayed the stories of several young women condemned for their futile attempts to cover up an illegitimate birth. Thorn had ensured

---

* Of a similar age was Shadrack Smith, a Gypsy described as "near 60 years of age" when executed on 22 March 1762. He was convicted on the evidence of his own son of robbing a young woman in the Charlbury area, leading him to caution all parents "not to put their lives into the hands of their children" (*Jackson's*, 27 March 1762).

that Amy Jacob was required to face no such choice. In his own final moments, according to a broadside, "his crime was held in such odious detestation that during the execution of that dreadful sentence of offended justice not a tear of pity was extorted in the last moments of distress".

Fact or fiction at the Golden Ball?: Jonathan Bradford

→►◄←

One last Oxford execution for murder deserves a brief mention, partly because the bizarre circumstances of the case make it seem more like a work of fiction, but also because that may be exactly what it was! Certainly, the murder of which Jonathan Bradford was found guilty in 1736 was included among others of undoubted reality in *Cries of Blood, or Juryman's Monitor* in 1767, and it has also been accepted as fact in later publications, but there appears to be no actual contemporary evidence. Whatever, even if the peculiar circumstances might imply something just too ironic, just too poetical in its justice, to be true, its inclusion here will, I hope, assist anyone who might undertake any further detective work in the future.

The gist of the story was that Christopher Hayes, a gentleman of Somerset, was travelling to Oxford to visit his uncle.* With night drawing in, he decided to lodge at a remote inn on the London road a few miles south of Oxford. There were two other

---

* Could he have been the Christopher Hayes who was baptised at Evercreech on 31 December 1673? Or his probable son, Christopher Hayes, who was apprenticed to a London vintner in 1720? There are also some other Somerset candidates, baptised at Dulverton in 1694 and Bridgewater in 1700.

guests that evening, and in conversation with them he unwisely let it be known that he had a large sum of money on him. Having overheard this, the landlord, Jonathan Bradford, stole into Hayes' room three times during the night, intending to steal the money. His resolve failed him on the first two occasions, but on the third, with his knife poised, he found that Hayes was "already murder'd and weltering in his blood". As he was searching Hayes' pockets, just in case the money had not been taken, the two other guests arrived on scene, having heard Hayes' groans of distress. It was instantly clear to them what must have happened, and they secured Bradford until the morning, when the local magistrate was summoned. On hearing the facts, he too was convinced of Bradford's culpability.

At "the ensuing assizes" Bradford was found guilty, and executed about a fortnight later.* During the trial, while admitting that he had indeed been tempted to steal Hayes' money, he persisted with the implausible story that he, like his other guests, had been awoken by the noise, and had merely taken the knife for his own protection. And yet, as it turned out, it was at least partly true! Some eighteen months later, on his death bed, and racked with guilt, Hayes' own servant confessed to the crime.†

The author of *Cries of Blood* stated that Bradford died "by all unpitied". There was much greater public sympathy and considerably

---

* This suggests that the murder was committed in June 1736, as elsewhere it was stated that Hayes was intending to stay in Oxford for the summer. Later accounts are suspiciously vague – including in *The Times* (8 January 1824) and *Oxford Times* (6 April 1878). It is the latter in which the inn is identified as the Golden Ball and also by the usually reliable Herbert Hurst in *Rambles and Rides around Oxford* (1885).

† Fictitious or not, the case *was* dramatised by Edward Fitzball as *Jonathan Bradford! Or The Murder at the Road-side Inn*, which was first performed in June 1833. It was summarised as factual in the *Complete Newgate Calendar* (1926), positioned between executions of December 1741 and March 1742.

more doubt apparent at the culmination of an investigation into a murder which occurred only a few miles from the Golden Ball later that century. To do justice to this notorious case, with its intriguing complexity, its revelations of a wide-ranging criminal underworld, the role of Daniel Harris, and its contentious outcome, the entire next chapter is devoted to "The Abingdon Water-turnpike Murder".

FIGURE 21 "View of Abingdon from Nuneham Park" by John and Josiah Boydell, published in 1794. The murder of David Charteris was perpetrated as he walked home in the direction of Nuneham through the fields to the left of the River Thames. Beyond is the Swift Ditch, where the waterturnpike public house stood.

CHAPTER SEVEN

THE ABINGDON WATERTURNPIKE MURDER OF 1787

"Being Moved and Seduced by the Instigation of the Devil"

When the Oxfordshire Coroner William Johnson examined the body of David Charteris on Thursday 11 October 1787, he was in no doubt about the cause of death. Charteris, an elderly linen trader from the village of Toot Baldon, had been discovered in a ditch near the River Thames, a little upstream of Abingdon, with his pockets emptied and "many marks of violence found on the head of him". In the standard phraseology of the time, Johnson concluded that Charteris had been robbed and murdered by some "evil disposed person or persons unknown, not having the fear of God before their eyes, but being moved and seduced by the instigation of the Devil".

The "horrid deed", as *Jackson's Oxford Journal* and the *Reading Mercury & Oxford Gazette* described it the same week, had been committed on the edge of Nuneham Park as Charteris was making his way home after attending Abingdon's annual Michaelmas Fair on the previous Monday. Paperwork retained by the local magistrate, Christopher Willoughby (c.1749–1808), provides a selective insight into the investigation that followed. From witness statements it was deduced that Charteris had been attacked a few minutes after leaving a public house by an old lock on what was then the main course of River Thames, known as Swift Ditch.* Attention focused on the obvious likely culprits: the other customers in the pub. But, as in all the best murder mysteries, the obvious turned out not to be the actual, and the tipplers in the Waterturnpike House that evening who had both the motive and the opportunity also had convincing alibis.

Indeed, it was nearly two and a half years before any further evidence was forthcoming. In March 1790, however, a coincidence of unguarded conversations and the unrelated arrest of an associate, the horse-thief Thomas Smith or Davis (that is, "Oxford Tom" – see Chapter 8) brought four Abingdon men into the frame. They were a sack-weaver called Richard Kilby (1764?–?); a Thames bargeman, John Castle (1759?–1790); a labourer, Giles Freeman Covington (1767–1791); and a former publican, Charles Evans Shury (1747–1790).

Soon after Smith's arrest, *Jackson's* made it known that he was intending to try to mitigate his expected capital sentence "by giving every information in his power". John Castle must have realised that his own name was bound to be mentioned, and this seems likely to have been the trigger for his rash admission to some fellow bargemen in Goring that he knew something about the Charteris

---

* The seventeenth-century lock is still visible on Swift Ditch, which at the time was the main navigation branch of the River Thames.

murder. Inevitably within a close-knit community which not only shared the same restricted, riverine geography, but also, to a large extent, the same genes, the rumour spread rapidly via the cabins of boats, busy wharves, noisy waterside bars, and bankside homes to reach the ears of the authorities in Oxford 30 miles upstream. Daniel Harris, the Oxford gaoler, was in the perfect position to act. His extensive involvement in new works on the river would inevitably have brought him into contact with the most influential river families, and in addition he worshipped at St Thomas' Church, the religious hub for Oxford's boating community. There was probably no-one better placed to round up those members of that community who were "in the know".

One by one the men implicated by Thomas Smith were arrested and brought to Oxford Castle. Richard Kilby was the first, in May 1790, and despite the fact that Smith had failed to save his own neck by turning King's evidence, Kilby trusted that he might be more fortunate: he revealed in detail not only the circumstances of several thefts of horses but also of the murder of David Charteris on that October evening two and a half years earlier. Kilby already had a criminal record, being described when found guilty of theft in 1784 as a man of "ill name and ill fame", yet in the absence of any other credible witnesses it was he on whom the Crown depended for their prosecution. He was ultimately pardoned and provided with the means to begin a new life in a new county.

Named now by both Smith and Kilby, the next man to be arrested was Charles Evans Shury, the evident ringleader. Shury was not the type of individual who might be expected to be prepared to kill a vulnerable old man for even the small change in his pocket: he was a prominent citizen from an old-established and prosperous Abingdon family. Indeed, his older brother John (1745–1804) could count himself among the wealthiest men in the town, having inherited their father's brewery in 1771 and married Elizabeth, the only daughter of a wealthy Oxford innkeeper, Francis White.

The two Shury brothers' early years show striking similarities, such that by mid-1773, while still both in their twenties, they were both widowers with daughters for whom they were responsible. But that is where their fates diverged. John made another advantageous marriage, but Charles wed himself to the bottle, it is safe to assume, as alcohol played a part in every one of the many petty crimes in which he was involved over a period of years. In October 1787, the time of the murder, the Shury family owned many substantial properties in Abingdon, and Charles ran the Chequer Inn in the centre of town. It was here that the others – Kilby, Castle, and Covington – would assemble and, fortified with Dutch Courage, would then venture into the night. Their stolen plunder – often no more valuable than chickens or pigeons – was then delivered to Shury for onward disposal or consumption.

In June 1790 John Castle joined Shury in Oxford Castle. Kilby was probably being held elsewhere for his own safety. He had attempted to flee, necessitating the circulation of a description:

> Worked as a bargeman and is well known by the West Country bargemen working in the Oxford & Abingdon boats to and from London. About 5 feet 4 inches high. Fit and strong-made, his complexion fair, thin visage and light sandy hair, a stiff sandy beard, light grey eyes, pocked nose and little pitted with the smallpox; mostly wears a blue bargeman's jacket and blue breeches.

The very nature of Castle's profession would have been enough to induce many at the time to make a premature judgement. With a widespread reputation for anti-social behaviour of all kinds, any bargeman would have found it especially difficult to invoke that cornerstone of English law, a presumption of innocence before proof of guilt. Indeed, some of the information revealed by Castle in his own failed attempt to earn a reprieve rather substantiated the prejudice, as he was persuaded to name numerous fellow bargemen involved in pilferage from Thames barges. But then, he also exposed a comparable number of culpable Abingdon citizens willing to accept the resultant stolen booty, and the impression grows with every testimony that very few residents of Abingdon in the 1780s were completely immune to temptation!

However, the nature of Castle's family situation at the end of 1787 makes the bargeman stereotype of an incorrigible, unprincipled villain seem less likely. When we learn, for instance, that he had been recently widowed, and left with three young children to care for, it is possible to see how desperate times might lead a poor man to desperate measures. Kilby made it clear that Castle was the least culpable of them all in the murder. It was to no avail. The "final exit of Shury and Castle" followed the Oxford assizes of July 1790.

Jackson's of 24 July and the *Reading Mercury & Oxford Gazette* of 26 July carried identical accounts:

> They were brought out of the chapel about half past eight in the morning, and having ascended the tower over the gateway they alternately harangued the multitude, confessing to having led wicked and dissolute lives, which they attributed to having been corrupted by bad company, but both positively denied the crime for which they were going to suffer. They also spoke to several persons whom they distinguished in the crowd beneath, though they were at the elevation of thirty three feet from the ground, and their general behaviour was hardened and vindictive in the

highest degree. A little before the execution, Castle dropped a letter, directed to William Bossom, written for him by one of the prisoners, the purport of which was to charge Bossom* with having borne false testimony upon the trial; and Shury called to another telling him he would go out like the snuff of a candle, as would his whole family.

This comment says much about Shury. Threatening retribution to the last would seem to confirm that his reputation was such that few people would dare cross him. In a town with a population of about 4,000, at a time when few people found reason to move far from their place of birth, many Abingdon residents would have been inter-related. It is quite possible that a conspiracy of silence explains the long delay in apprehending those responsible for what was an initially well-publicised murder, occurring on a busy public holiday on a public footpath. The common logic of the time was probably that the benefits of reporting a guilty person to the authorities were unlikely to justify the potential retribution of that person's many nearby friends or relatives – especially if the accusation proved false. It is a not-uncommon scenario to this day. On this occasion, once the culprits were safely behind bars, a large number of witnesses did suddenly come forward!

Whatever his true nature, one can only admire Shury's ability to retain a sense of humour to the end. The "gallows speech" was expected additional entertainment for the onlookers, and Shury did not disappoint. Castle too had plenty to say – too much, in Shury's opinion. After proclaiming, "My Boys! God bless you. I am as innocent as a lamb of what I am going to suffer for, so God

---

* The Bossoms were one of the principal boating families of Oxford, as mentioned in Chapter 4.

forgive you all!", he encouraged the executioner to hasten to "turn them off or that fellow would keep talking all the day". Both men's bodies were delivered to the University for anatomical lectures.*

Meanwhile, Giles Freeman Covington, the youngest of the gang, had gone on the run, on account of which this description was issued:

> Aged about 20 years, born at Abingdon, has lived there ever since, five feet nine inches high, very stout and well made, flaxen hair, pale complexion, light grey eyes, long visage, large, long nose, remarkably gruff in speech, mostly wears a blue coat with white metal buttons, white linen waistcoat, brown corduroy breeches, walks very upright, rather swaggering in his gait.

He too merits little compassion at first glance. After his capture in January 1791, largely due to the efforts of two of John Fielding's Bow Street men, the newspapers had no intention of waiting for the formality of a trial to condemn him as "an atrocious offender". Yet in all likelihood he was not the iniquitous individual that the authorities wanted the public to believe, but more a gullible youth whom Shury had recruited for his powerful physique. As the *Reading Mercury & Oxford Gazette* noted: "He is a remarkable stout fellow, and was deemed an excellent pugilist."

Covington's father, Roger (1729–1798), had moved to Abingdon from London as a young man. There he raised a family, lived a virtuous and industrious life as a tailor, and assumed the prestigious and responsible civic role of Bellman in 1780. His three oldest sons benefited from precious apprenticeships, and rose to become

---

* Another man implicated by Smith was James Williams – see Chapter 8 – who was tried at the same summer assizes as Shury and Castle, but hanged two weeks later.

reputable Abingdon tradesmen; Giles, however, rose only as far as the gallows above the entrance to Oxford Castle. The parish records tell a sad yet timeless tale of teenage rebelliousness – a story shaped by the circumstances of the time, yet in some ways as familiar as last week. In December 1787, just two months after the murder, Giles' illegitimate daughter was baptised, to the absolute horror of his respectable and respected father, no doubt. He married the recently-orphaned mother, Ann Gilkes, in February 1789; they had a short-lived son, Gyles, while in hiding in London (where numerous Covington relatives still resided) in May 1790; their daughter died of smallpox the following August; and then Ann herself died, in September 1791, only a few months after her husband's execution. Here is the chronology of a behind-the-scenes tragedy which adds weight to a view of Covington as loving and loyal, imprudent and impetuous, but hardly "atrocious".

Covington had attempted to escape justice by joining the Navy, where, on board a warship called the *London*, he excelled, being "so regular and attentive to his duty as to be rated an able seaman much earlier than is usual with persons who have never before been at sea". However, "at sea" was not where he could stay indefinitely, and when the *London* docked at Spithead on 2 January 1791, a Bow Street officer called Jealous (the same man, presumably, who had arrested Joseph Simmonds in 1783 – see Chapter 3) was waiting to escort him to Oxford under heavy guard.

At his trial at the 1791 Lent assizes it was essentially Covington's word versus that of Kilby, making the verdict a foregone conclusion. In accordance with statute, he was executed on the Monday after the trial. The reports in both *Jackson's* of 12 March and the *Gazette* of two days later were identical save for one highly significant paragraph. Thomas "Oxford Tom" Smith had used his last few moments to speak out in repentance; Shury and Castle in recrimination. If this kind of additional entertainment was expected of Covington, he disappointed. All the papers had to say was that he was executed at about a quarter to ten

> upon the tower at the entrance to our Castle … in the presence of a prodigious multitude of spectators. He came upon the scaffold dressed in his sailor's jacket and trowsers, with white gloves and a white hatband, and although he had summoned up all his fortitude, he was nevertheless pale as a corpse, and exceedingly agitated. Having mounted the drop, he threw over a paper which he desired might be read aloud, yet without attempting to say more, forthwith gave the signal, and the executioner did his office.

The popular appeal of executions encouraged a market for eye-witness accounts of notorious cases. Covington's qualified, and a broadside was printed with the title of "A true and authentic account of the trial and dying behaviour of Giles Covington". The writer's opinion about Covington's "dying behaviour" was very different from that of the newspapers. Far from being "exceedingly agitated", this version was that he "maintained an undaunted resolution to the last", which accords with the opinion that Daniel Harris expressed in a private letter to Christopher Willoughby, that his behaviour had been "decent and becoming in every particular excepting his not acknowledging the murder".

The newspapers discounted Covington's protestations of innocence, concluding their accounts with a typical appeal to the moral sensibilities of the reader, saying:

> We have only to lament the wickedness and depravity of human nature, that any hardened wretches should thus dare, in their dying

moments, by attempting to impose upon credulous minds, insult an already offended deity.

This unwavering condemnation would have been very much to the authorities' satisfaction, in view of its likely influence on those people still unconvinced of the justice of the verdict. And there were plenty of them, as Daniel Harris informed Willoughby, saying there "could be no secrecy observed ... for I hear tis generally spoken of up town". He was referring to the hugely significant additional text that the *Gazette* had included but the Oxford paper had not: the very letter that Covington had thrown down from the scaffold. Its contents did nothing to appease the doubtful, especially in view of the suspicion that it cast on the Crown's star witness.

> What I have now to say cannot be of any further service to me in this world, than by affording me the satisfactory reflection of having done my duty for the few remaining hours I have to stay in it. For that purpose, I have made a full confession of my transgressions and errors, to prevent others from being blamed for what I have committed. There only remains now for me to do justice to myself, by solemnly and truly declaring, in the presence of Almighty God, my entire innocence of the transaction for which I now suffer. My prosecutors and false accusers I pardon sincerely; but I caution all young and unthinking people from forming any connections, or keeping company with Kilby, or the other two who have falsely sworn away my life, lest, for their own purposes, they should take advantage of an unwary heart, and bring them into the same calamity, which has undeservedly fallen upon me.

Covington had addressed a similar, but much less grammatical, letter direct to Christopher Willoughby. (It was retained by him

among his personal papers, edited below for easier comprehension.)
It expressed the same sentiments of selfless concern, in the context
of a resigned but determined plea of innocence.

> Sir, I have to trouble you with these few lines concerning this horrid
> affair which I am in Oxon Castle for, or at least which is laid to my
> charge. There is no doubt, Sir, you been at a deal of trouble about
> it and a deal of expense, but, Sir Willabe, how happy tis for me to
> go to this untimely end, which I expect in a short time, and to call
> God to be a witness, and here to deny it for me, which I can with a
> safe conscience, I thank God for it.
>
> There is no doubt but the poor man lost his life, but, Sir Willabe,
> it not found out it, and so you'd find when 'tis too late for me. But
> it not only, Sir, taking my life. There is the poor widow that will be
> left to God and the wide world, and my poor mother and father
> with sorrow to their graves, but the how to make their selfs happy,
> more so than if I had been guilty of it, which I am not, I thank God.
>
> I hope you and your family will live to find that Giles Freeman
> Covington died innocent, and then I hope you will relieve the
> widow that left behind if Bedlam is not her doom, instead of
> putting my life, being gone, which shall be of no further service. So
> no more from the unfortunate youth, Giles Freeman Covington. I
> hope God will be with you and yours.

Covington had seemingly been far more riled than the others by
Kilby's treachery. He never denied being present when the murder
was committed, but was genuinely indignant at the role that Kilby,
and only Kilby, allotted him in the drama. Covington's very public
resentment of Kilby would soon be widely talked of – and not
only locally. The London broadside writer picked up on this theme
too, and Daniel Harris had a similar recollection. In his letter to

Willoughby he reported that Covington "spoke not a word upon the scaffold, but threw down a paper which expressed that he had left behind a full confession of all his offences, but that he was innocent of what he was going to suffer for, concluding beware of Kilby".

With Covington dead, only one man knew what really happened that October evening three and a half years earlier: Richard Kilby. And of all the main characters in this tale, it is Kilby alone who eludes positive identification in the parish registers – but perhaps that is the hallmark of the accomplished informer to vanish with few traces! The Abingdon Waterturnpike Murder could well have been a case of eighteenth-century justice being seen to be done, rather than *actually* being done. There were probably many more cases like it, and for any reader with a murderer in their distant family past, it may be consoling to think that among county or parish archives another, more honourable, version of their story might be waiting to be told.*

---

* The paperwork retained by Christopher Willoughby (Oxfordshire History Centre Wi/VI/iv) was crucial to piecing together the chronology of this case, investigated in detail in *The Abingdon Waterturnpike Murder* (2008). After dissection, Covington's skeleton was retained by the University. Labelled merely as "Englishman" for decades, he was then exhibited at the Museum of Oxford until modern sensibilities dictated that such a display was inappropriate.

CHAPTER EIGHT

EXECUTIONS (2)

Of Highwaymen, Horse-Thieves, Burglars, and Counterfeiters

In the cases of murder outlined in Chapter 6, familial intimacy between perpetrator and victim was a common factor. Occasionally, however, members of the same family were *united* in committing a lesser crime still deemed worthy of capital punishment, and this chapter begins with the stories of two sets of brothers whose lives all ended on the Oxford Castle gallows.

The brothers Williams and Cox

On Monday 28 August 1766, John Williams of Beckley and John Milward (alias Brown) from Northamptonshire were hanged at Oxford for highway robbery. In the previous March they had robbed Mrs Rachel Newell of Stokenchurch of nearly ten guineas one evening as she travelled between her home and West Wycombe (in Buckinghamshire). Both young men, they had known each

other for only a matter of days, and claimed that this was the only crime of any consequence that they had ever committed. Often youth was seen as an extenuating circumstance, deserving of the reprieve of transportation or military enlistment, but Milward and Williams were not so fortunate. At their execution, Milward met every expectation of the crowd in providing a spirited speech from the gallows. *Jackson's Oxford Journal* reported that he "harangued the populace for some time", saying that "Sabbath-breaking and bad company had brought upon them their present misfortunes", and "begging that their dreadful example might be a warning to others". Indeed, with admirable aplomb, he delivered a surely tongue-in-cheek warning of his own: "that the age was indeed arrived at so high a pitch of wickedness ... that it was not uncommon for people who live by thieving to attend publick executions in order to pick pockets". No doubt gaining many new admirers with his performance, Milward "met his fate with great courage, shaking hands with many people near the cart, and desiring the prayers of the spectators".

Williams was much less forthcoming, albeit he too remained stoical. His mother had spent the previous few days begging for money for a coffin, and although she was successful in this depressing chore, she was unable to get it to the gallows in time – the location of the execution is not specified – and the ultimate fate of the corpse is unknown. If poor Mrs Williams had lived long

FIGURE 22 "View of the New County Prison at Abingdon, Berks.", engraved by H. Meyer from a drawing by William Watkin Waite. The ancient bridge over the Thames is that crossed by David Charteris on 8 October 1787, prior to his murder. In so doing, walking from right to left, he had crossed from Berkshire to Oxfordshire. The barge is similar to that on which one of the men executed for his murder, John Castle, would have worked. The prison, built to the design of Daniel Harris, was opened in 1811

FIGURE 23 "The New County Jail with the old Castle Tower, Oxford" as drawn by a pupil of the Oxford artist John Malchair in 1797. The view across New Road shows the main gate, above which executions were held within clear view of the public from 1787. [Copyright: Bodleian Library, University of Oxford. MS Top. Oxon. c299 f230]

enough to witness the execution of another of her sons, James, a full 24 years later, she would perhaps have found some small consolation in his greater volubility – even if his final words were of a touchingly mundane naivety.

James Williams was one of four men whose association with the habitual London horse-thief, Thomas "Oxford Tom" Smith (alias Davis), had fatal consequences (see Chapter 7). Smith's comprehensive confession prior to his own execution at Oxford in March 1790 occasioned the subsequent arrest and executions of the Abingdon men Charles Evans Shury and John Castle later that year, and of Giles Freeman Covington in 1791. James Williams was more directly associated with Smith than any of these men. Born in Beckley, he had worked for numerous farmers near Wheatley, Thame, and Bletchingdon over a period of twelve years or more until his then current employer, Thomas Busby of Bletchingdon, entrusted him to drive his sheep to Smithfield market in London. Described by *Jackson's* as "rather more ignorant in many respects than is even common to labouring men", Williams pocketed the money, and never returned.

Several years later Williams made the acquaintance of "Oxford Tom" at Moorfields, and within five weeks the two men contrived to steal a mare, saddle, and colt from one of Williams' former employers, Thomas Juggins of Wheatley. This was early in 1790, and their subsequent arrest was due, not so much to the efforts of the hard-pressed forces of law and order, but to Juggins' own determination to reclaim his property. *Jackson's* of 3 April 1790 praised him (and another victim of Smith's predilection for other people's horses, Simon Peck of Rye Farm near Abingdon) for his "laudable spirit, almost regardless of either fatigue or expense" in bringing Williams and Smith to justice. Williams was in fact already, "in the thieves' phrase, *at home*, being in Clerkenwell prison for stealing a saddle", but was brought to Oxford to be tried for the more serious theft of Juggins' mare. Found guilty, Williams seemed quite unaffected at his execution on Monday 2 August 1790, according to a broadside, and continued to protest his innocence. His last words were quoted as: " 'My boys, take warning, for I am just going! But my cap will blow off, won't it?', and in that hardened state of insensitivity the poor wretch was launched into eternity". The loss of his headgear would have been the least of his worries, one would have thought!

Whereas a gap of more than two decades separated the executions of the two Williams brothers, the other siblings executed at Oxford, John and Richard Cox, died together, in literally touching circumstances. John (31) and Richard (21) Cox were members of what *Jackson's* called "a gang of villains who have long infested Henley and its neighbourhood". They were found guilty of stealing lead and sheep through the revelations of John Perrin, an accomplice, who, unwisely and unusually, "kept a regular journal of their transactions for a series of years".

The brothers were not alone on the scaffold on Monday 27 March 1786. With them were Miles Ward and John Grace, making this the largest known number of simultaneous executions at Oxford. Grace (24) had also been found guilty of stealing sheep; Ward (21) of the theft of silverware from the chapel of Magdalen College. At the execution,

> Ward behaved himself in a manner very suitable to his situation; he prayed fervently and shed tears abundantly, yet with a becoming firmness; Grace and the elder Cox shewed also a proper sense of the near approach of death, but the younger of the Coxes seemed

either hardened or stupefied in his last moments. When all four, standing up in the cart, were tied up to the gallows, Ward, with great composure, asked his companions *Are you all ready to die? If you are, let us take leave of one another.* They then all shook hands, and the cart drawing away before the brothers had quitted each other's hold, they long remained with the hands of each strongly clasped together.*

Perhaps the youngest person to have been executed in Oxford was James Till. Described as about 17 in *Jackson's,* but "no more than 16 years of age" by the London *Public Advertiser,* he was hanged on Friday 26 April 1754 for stealing between 62 and 70 guineas from his employer, after two attempts for a pardon failed. The following week, *Jackson's* printed a letter from an unnamed University source. The writer stated that Till's body was "regularly delivered to the gentlemen of the University for the purpose of anatomical lectures" without incident. This was attributed to the presence of "several stout, resolute persons … with orders to lay hold of, and secure in the castle, any person or persons who should make the least attempt towards carrying off the body". This measure had been deemed prudent on account of the rioters who had made off with two executed bodies about a month previously (i.e. Acton Brice and Richard Bayliss).

There were some 30 people known to have been executed for theft, of either livestock, money, or goods, at Oxford Castle in the

---

* There had been no executions in Oxford during the previous two years, and perhaps the only other public spectacle capable of attracting thousands of spectators had occurred in November 1784. This was the air-balloon ascent by the Oxford pastry cook and "first English aeronaut", James Sadler. Nationally, these aeronautical events became a magnet for pick-pockets. When Sadler made a triumphant return to ballooning in Oxford in 1810 seven notorious thieves from London and Birmingham were arrested by two Bow Street officers, and held at the castle.

eighteenth century, and about half as many for highway robbery. The latter was a crime which grew through the century to be imbued with a romance which, if the highwayman exhibited sufficient civility, charm, or gallantry to his victims, accorded the perpetrators a degree of admiration unknown to the petty thief or fraudster. By far the most celebrated highwayman to be executed in Oxford was Isaac Darkin (alias Dumas).

"Joy to thee, lovely thief!": Isaac Darkin(g), alias Dumas

-+>-<+-

Although Darkin was only 20 when he died, his fame was such that two lengthy versions of his life were published soon after. The details that follow are taken mainly from *Jackson's* and, in respect of his early life, from a pamphlet printed specifically for William Jackson (and endorsed by William Wisdom, the gaoler) entitled *The Authentic Trial and Memoirs of Isaac Darkin alias Dumas*.

Darkin was born the son of a cork-cutter in London's Eastcheap district in about 1740. When his father died in about 1754, Darkin and his step-sister ran the business together for about three years. At this point Darkin – who "shewed marks of genius and abilities sufficient to have procured him the respect of mankind" but whose "researches were rather after what is called a *Knowledge of the Town*" and who had decided that "the reputation of a *Bon Companion* was far more desirable than that of *a reputable tradesman*" – was drawn to a life of crime, in order to support a lifestyle of great extravagance and many mistresses. He enjoyed nine months of success in the Essex area, but was eventually apprehended for a highway robbery. Initially sentenced to hang, he was reprieved on account of his youth on condition that he serve in the army, and was dispatched to Antigua in January 1759. There he proved "much superior in capacity to the people who are generally met with in the station", and although he struggled with the discipline (being court-martialled three times in seven weeks), he was sufficiently personable to be appointed to a relatively undemanding role as the servant of an officer.

However, Darkin yearned for home. Somehow he persuaded the captain of a merchant ship to smuggle him back to England, even though this offence carried a penalty of £100, and he was back on English soil about nine months after his departure. He immediately resumed his old ways, adopting now the alias of Dumas (and also Harris and Hamilton); but when he realised that he was suspected he found a solution common among men on the run: the Navy. Darkin was no ordinary fugitive, however. He found that seamanship gave him not a new direction in life, but excellent cover to pursue his old one, and he continued to commit robberies while on furloughs from his ship, the *Royal George*. These crimes were committed in Somerset, Nottinghamshire, Leicestershire, Gloucestershire, Northamptonshire, and Wiltshire. In the latter county, he was arrested and tried for the robbery on 22 June 1760 of Lord Percival, but found not guilty. Even though it was clearly proven that it was his gun that had been used, he convinced the jury that it had been stolen from him before the robbery had occurred.

Soon after his release he was at it again, this time selecting victims in various parts of Oxfordshire – he passed through Banbury, Bloxham, Burford, Chipping Norton, Lechlade, Walling-ford, and Wantage – before depriving a Smithfield apothecary, Robert Gammon, of a gold watch and money on the highway near Nettlebed. This time his identity was not in much doubt, and pressure was exerted on one of his lovers, Polly Cannon, who revealed the location of his lodgings in Smithfield. He was arrested there by William Marsden, one of the unofficial network of "thief-takers" employed by Sir John Fielding, who had been on his case for some three years. Darkin was then taken to Newgate gaol, before being transferred to Oxford Castle in January 1761 to stand trial at the following assizes.

Jackson's was especially adoring when reporting his imminent arrival from London, describing him as "a lively and facetious companion, and is said to sing an excellent song, on which account we hope the governor will accommodate him with an elegant apartment, for the more commodious exhibition of his agreeable talents". This might be interpreted as irony, but the following week, *Jackson's* reported visits "by many gentlemen of the University of all ranks and degrees", and with apparent genuine approval added that many of them "in consideration of his proper deportment under his present unhappy circumstances, have generously contributed to relieve the expenses and anxieties of a tedious confinement". Evidently, a rumour spread that among these contributions were a University cap and gown intended to disguise an escape, because William Wisdom was later obliged to deny this (in a notice of 18 April 1761).

Darkin's defence was weak, based essentially on having not prepared one! Earlier that March day he had "behaved with much unconcern, kissing all the girls that came to see him; and as he was a smart fellow, there were many of them in love with him". He was popular with his own sex too, and had fully anticipated an adjournment on the basis of the influence of the scholars "whose curiosity and free behaviour to him in the castle ... he had idly construed into some regard for his person, and thought, let the worst come that could come, he should get a pardon by their means". He did not, nor was he granted any extra time to prepare a defence, and on this occasion there was no reprieve. Almost all the scholars had been ejected from the court beforehand, "the rumour of a rescue being echoed from every corner", and none was permitted to attend the execution early in the morning of Monday 23 March.

The New College undergraduate James Woodforde, who had previously visited him in the castle on the 2 February, noted in his diary on the appointed day: "All the College gates was shut from ten o'clock last night till nine this morning." On the day before, according to *Jackson's*, he had chosen as his final reading matter the *Beggar's Opera*, and "appeared to enter thoroughly into the spirit of Mackheath's part, and seemed greatly to enjoy the character".* Dashing to the last, Darkin had

> a taste for elegance in every respect, was remarkably fond of silk stockings, and neat in his linnen, had his hair dressed in the most fashionable manner every morning, his polished fetters were supported round his waist by a sword belt, and tied up at the knees with ribbon,

causing a clergyman to regret that "Mr. Darkin studied more to appear like a Gentleman than a Penitent Christian". His wardrobe on the day of the execution was also described: a mourning suit comprising a striped waistcoat under a black one, with a clean ruffled shirt. After he had received the holy sacrament, "one of the prisoners that was to be hangman was called in" and accompanied

---

* John Gay's musical play opened in January 1728, and became the biggest musical hit of the eighteenth century. It tells of the relationship between a highwayman, Captain Macheath, and the daughter of a thief-taker, Polly Peachum.

Darkin to the ladder, where he knelt and prayed, before ascending it quickly. Then he

> pulled off his neckcloth, unbuttoned the collar of his shirt and waistcoat, and put the rope about his neck. Then pulling a white handkerchief out of his pocket, which he tied over his face, and several times asking the populace to hang upon him, he turned his back to the ladder, and himself fixing the rope, in a moment dropped his neckcloth as a signal, but without waiting for the ladder's being turned, stepped off.

It was not perhaps the dramatic, entertaining finale expected of such a charismatic figure, but it was at least a dignified one. Another account, the *Genuine Life of Isaac Darking alias Dumas,* recorded in corroboration that "after the fatal cord was fastened, he turned himself off, with some eagerness, to explore the unfathomable gulph of eternity". Newspapers were often generous in their praise of those facing execution with penitence and dignity. In Darkin's case, *Jackson's* verged on hero worship, saying that "his behaviour in his last moments was entirely correspondent to the steadiness of character and intrepidity which he affected and maintained even in his most dangerous enterprises". The body remained hanging for nearly an hour and was then taken "in triumph" to St Thomas' Church by bargemen, according to *Jackson's*, and "most inhumanly mangled, in order to prevent (according to his request) his being anatomised". The author of *Genuine Life* provided more precise details, saying that Darkin had left the bargemen five guineas

> to save him from the hands of surgeons who waited for his body in order to dissect it. But to render their design abortive, the bargemen cut open his body, took out his bowels, and filled it with lime.

This gruesome outcome caused *Jackson's* to muse that "could he have foreseen this treatment, he would perhaps have shewn less reluctance". William Jackson's authorised *Authentic Trial and Memoirs* added a further ghoulish detail: that the bargemen then "opened the grave where Grindey was buried, who was hanged some years ago for returning from transportation, and buried him in that coffin".*

It was a gruesome end for a young man who had captured the public imagination with his daring exploits, his decent behaviour, and beguiling charm. Many a female tear was probably shed at the time. In *Genuine Life*, Darkin's attitude was summarised as being that "a highwayman without a whore was as uncouth as a knight without a lady", but before his death he had expressed the contrary hope that "he should not see any women among the spectators, as that would affect him greatly, for they had been his ruin". He was not the first or last condemned man to express such sentiments, but for Darkin the association was undeniable. The writer of *Authentic Trial and Memoirs* claimed that during his confinement at Salisbury, where he had used the alias of John Dumas,

> his sufferings made a deep impression upon the tender hearts of the ladies, some of whom having visited him in his confinement, his obliging manner, genteel address, lively disposition, and whole deportment, so struck them that his fame soon became the discourse of the tea table.

One consequence was this verse, the first of five composed by "certain

---

* William Grindy, a former innkeeper of Nettlebed according to one newspaper source, was committed to Oxford Castle on 5 August 1752 "for returning from transportation before time expired". He was given the death penalty at his trial on 9 March 1753, and executed therefore probably on Monday 12th.

belles who visited him in prison", but who, the author observed with the advantage of hindsight, were "not good at prognostication"!

> Joy to thee, lovely thief! That thou
> Hast 'scap'd the fatal string.
> Let gallows groan with ugly rogues
> Dumas must never swing.

"Plunderings and devastations": William Hyde of Stanton St John

Isaac Darkin differs from most other men and women executed at Oxford in being someone who was sufficiently capable and well educated to have forged a successful career of a legitimate nature. Another man in a similar mould was William Hyde or Hide, one of Oxfordshire's more intriguing home-grown criminals of the period. Hyde is a classic example of a talented man who squandered all for the lack of a little willpower. Born at Stanton St John in about 1746, Hyde was a bright child and had soon mastered his father's trade of sieve-making, "in which employment", according to a broadside of his life, "he was equalled by few and excelled by none; nay so excellent were his talents that there are very few handycraft trades in which he did not exhibit wonderful abilities". He was also "an excellent tinker, basket maker and chair maker, a good cobbler, and one of the very best hands in the husbandry business this day in *England*". Furthermore "in the employment of hedging, ditching and planting of beans, or hoeing of turnips, he would alone do as much as any two men in the country".

One might suspect a degree of bias in such a fulsome appraisal, akin to the propagandist intentions of the earlier broadside about the Barton murderer John Protheroe, perhaps, but the writer continues to suggest that all this industry was merely "a cover for his rogueries". These included two instances of "unlawfully lopping, and otherwise damaging certain timber trees in the woods" belonging to St John's College near Stanton St John, for which he was sentenced to a total of 18 months' imprisonment inside Oxford Castle. Three of those months, however, were spent in the marines, an alternative penance that he clearly regretted, since he took the drastic measure of cutting off his own right thumb in order to obtain a discharge.

Immediately on his release in May 1777, Hyde abandoned his wife and four children in order to abscond with a petty thief called Mary Makemalt.* On 19 October that year the pair decided to burgle an empty house in Old Cutteslowe, and in a wanton display of cheek "regaled themselves not only with eggs and bacon, but had also beat up some batter, fried pancakes, and supplied themselves plentifully from the cellar". It was probably the last good meal that Hyde ever digested! Both he and Makemalt were apprehended and taken to the castle to await the March assizes. He received the death penalty, but she appears to have been excused. There are hints of a tangled love-life in the fact that the principal evidence against the pair (surely in the spirit of a jilted lover?) was one Mary Allen, described as another of Hyde's "pillow companions".

On the Saturday before the execution Hyde was visited by

---

* Hyde's wife's name was Hannah, and their children were Mary, baptised at Stanton St John in 1767, Elizabeth in 1769, Patience in 1773, and Phoebe in 1775. Hyde, spelled Hide, is presumably the son baptised by William and Martha Hide on 21 July 1746 – even though the broadside gave his year of birth as 1749.

his mother and neighbours from Stanton. Unless they had come to gloat, these, presumably, were not the same neighbours who apparently "dreaded his appearance near their habitations, for his departure was generally attended by a discovery of plunderings and devastations"! Friends came too, and when it was suggested to Hyde that rather than converse with so many visitors "his mind might be more collected and his time better spent by withdrawing to the chapel, he replied with great composure that the chapel was a very cold place". He retained his impudent calm to the end, which came on Monday 22 March 1779, his undoubted talent wasted simply for a self-confessed weakness for "Sabbath-breaking, loose company and drunkenness".

The "reformed mode" of execution

Until the end of the eighteenth century the public was rarely prevented from gathering close to the gallows, whether at Green Ditch or the Castle Green, so that the requests made by Isaac Darkin and Anne Green, for instance, for someone to pull down on their legs to hasten the moment of death, could be fairly easily accomplished. It was in any case considered to be efficacious to touch the corpse of an executed person, or to purchase their clothing or a piece of the rope (a customary additional reward for the hangman), as previously stated. Add to that the contrary motives of claimants of the corpse, and a little disquiet was almost inevitable – at least until 1787, when, on account of the design of the rebuilt prison, such scenes became a thing of the past. With the gallows placed some 30 feet above the ground, on top of the new main gateway overlooking New Road (see Figure 23), Oxford's anatomists and surgeons could sharpen their knives with rather greater confidence.

The first men to experience this elevated place of execution were Thomas White and Charles Walter Wyatt, both of whom had succumbed to temptations arising from their respective employments. White had stolen various items of silverware from Blenheim Palace while employed as footman to the Duchess of Marlborough, and Wyatt had embezzled public funds while apprenticed to the Post Master at Witney. Although not connected in any way, both men had fled to London when detected and both were apprehended by the capital's Bow Street Runners, representing notable early successes for John Fielding's fledgling police force.

The pair were hanged together on Monday 6 August 1787. The novelty of the "reformed mode" of execution, so very much more visible to the public than ever before, inspired *Jackson's* to an unusually generous number of column inches. At four o'clock in the morning both men were summoned to the chapel, to be informed only then that the execution would be that same day, but that they could choose the moment themselves, at any time between 8am and 12 noon. This lack of warning seems rather odd, in that it would mean that relatively few people would witness the event, when the prevailing rationale was to demonstrate to as many people as possible that crime did not pay. Perhaps it was deemed sensible, on this first occasion above the gateway, to suppress public interest in case of any unforeseen difficulties. Whatever, the two men opted to postpone the fatal moment for as long as possible. At 7am, they were attended by the castle chaplain, and at 9am "prisoners of every description" attended divine service. A strict fast was observed, and no work was permitted at the gaol for the whole day. At 11am, White's and Wyatt's fetters were removed and the sacrament administered, after which the debtors returned to their apartments, while the other prisoners remained in the felons' yard (this being the other main innovation: that all the other convicts should be obliged to witness and, it was hoped, heed, the occasion).

At 12 noon, the two men were taken from the chapel to the gallows with due respect for ceremony. The procession consisted of six of the sheriff's men "with javelins, two and two, the executioner, bareheaded, the two malefactors, in white caps and pinioned, between the turnkeys, armed, Redditch, a condemned criminal, but reprieved, guarded by two constables, the rest of the felons, two and two, also guarded".* To add to the sense of occasion, the bell of St Thomas' Church "tolled upwards of an hour and a half before and during the execution".

The executions of White and Wyatt were the first to occur during the tenure of Daniel Harris as governor. The last (making 18 in all) was also a notable one, on account of the preserved detail of the procedure on that day, and also the fact that the man in question was, for the first verifiable time, permitted to be interred within the castle grounds.

---

* Thomas Redditch was presumably being given a close-up demonstration of the narrowness of his escape – unless in fact he is named because he was the hangman that day. He remained incarcerated with hard labour until at least 1790.

"The prison is a palace today": Thomas Davis

✦✦✦

Thomas Davis was aged 43 when he died in 1805, convicted of "having uttered a counterfeited note, purporting to be a one pound note ... with intent to defraud Elizabeth Cecil of Chipping Norton".* Born in Droitwich (Worcs.), Davis was a religious dissenter, and it is the account of "the respectable minister of that society in this city", James Hinton, from which much of this intimate detail comes, in the form of a long printed letter entitled *A Narrative of the Behaviour and Death of Thomas Davis.*† Davis had had scant religious instruction in his life and was convinced that this was the cause of his downfall, because "evil company, Sabbath-breaking and gaming had first led him from the paths of virtue". Hinton convinced him that with true repentance it was not too late for spiritual salvation, however. Davis' final weeks were therefore conducted with greater cheer than for most who awaited death within the castle's condemned cell, even if one cannot help but feel that Hinton – who, to be fair, waited until 1811 to publish his account – might have been tempted to exaggerate the effectiveness of his ministrations. For instance, Hinton quotes Davis as saying at one point:

> I bless God night and day that I ever entered the walls of this prison. The little hope I feel that I shall obtain mercy gives a happiness to

---

* Counterfeiting was, with murder, arson, and treason, one of the 200 or so capital offences for which leniency was rarely shown.

† Prison chaplains, or "ordinaries" as they were also called, were often the source of the broadsides published after executions, this being generally accepted as reasonable recompense for the spiritual succour provided.

which none of the pleasure of sin can ever be compared. I never knew anything like happiness till now.

His morale was sustained to the last. On the day before the execution, Hinton joined him and two relatives in prayer, sitting on the coffin in his cell as there was no other seat. Afterwards Davis said: "The prison is a palace today; this is surely somewhat like to Heaven. Do not let us weep any more. O! Blessed be God, for giving such a Sabbath as this for my last." Hinton stayed with Davis throughout the night. At 5am, workmen began to erect the platform. Hinton felt that "every stroke of the hammer reached my heart, but poor Davis heard the noise close to his cell without dismay". At 6.30am both men walked to the chapel "which is at a short distance, and on the flat roof of which the platform as usual was erected". Soon after

the executioner entered. He was attended by the proper officers, and he held out in his hand the *instrument of death*. A more terrific appearance I think no human form could assume. His keen eye rolled over the apartment in search of his victim. Davis calmly shook hands with him and said, "I am ready, do your duty."

Still in irons, Davis then ascended the long staircase to the scaffold unassisted. Hinton read out Davis' short admission of guilt and remorse, then retired. The broadside summarised the scene in front of an "immense" number of spectators, "the generality of which shewed that pathetic feeling and compassion due to a relenting penitent" who was

perfectly convinced that the hard earned shilling is far preferable to the guinea gained by fraudulence and deceit, and begs and most earnestly intreats all those who see or hear of his untimely death to be warned against that practice, and avoid avaricious desires, gambling, drinking, and all other baneful excesses, which lead on to speedy ruin and premature death, and entail a lasting disgrace on their memory, and an heart-breaking reflection to their innocent progeny.

The final act in this particularly poignant version of a familiar routine was described by *Jackson's* of 30 March 1805:

> The behaviour of the spectators was highly becoming the solemn occasion, and we understand that while the body was suspended, the prisoners who as usual witnessed the execution, were assembled in the chapel, and a very proper sermon preached to them, with great effect, by the regular chaplain. The body was immediately put in a coffin, which had been in the cell with him the whole of Sunday, and at his particular request, buried in a grave dug by his fellow prisoners, in the consecrated ground belonging to the chapel of St George within the walls of the castle.*

The last execution at Oxford for any crime other than murder occurred in 1832, when John Gibbs of Steeple Aston and George Lay of Abingdon were hanged simultaneously for arson and highway robbery respectively. The last public execution of all at Oxford was on 24 March 1863, five years before it was abolished as a public spectacle throughout the land. Noah Austin, a farmer's son from Upper Heyford, was hanged that day for murdering his lover's father.†

---

* *Jackson's* of 29 September 1798 mentions the consecration of "the new-built chapel of St George and burial ground within the walls of our Castle". Subsequently, several executed men were buried here, but it was not until 1836 that the first convicted murderer was admitted (see Appendix 1).

† A short, eye-witness account of this execution was reprinted from the *Oxford Times* in Thomas Squires' *In West Oxford* (1928). In *Oxford Yesterday*, W. E. Sherwood (1927) revealed the Victorian complacency with which the termination of life was accepted: "I can well remember the morbid curiosity with which I viewed the crowd and scaffold …, feeling defrauded that I must go on and answer my name at school just as the fatal hour was striking."

"Doing time" to leisure time

-+>-<+-

This has been an often uncomfortable history to write. In *A Proposal for Making Effectual Provision for the Poor* (1753), Henry Fielding wrote (just before his death): "The sufferings of the poor are indeed less observed than their misdeeds." This book is a humble attempt to rectify that situation a little. From a distance of many decades, it is sometimes possible to overlook the fact that the people whose suffering or misdeeds have been described were sentient, breathing human beings, rather than characters in a series of historical adventure stories.

From the evidence available, it is apparent that many of the prisoners described were luckless or desperate victims of circumstance, rather than malevolent or incorrigible miscreants. As a consequence, many who found themselves on the very public platform of the gallows were lauded by the masses as champions of the down-trodden, or as rebels against an overbearing system of law and morality. It became tempting to think of everyone who is featured in this book in these terms (especially in those cases where the establishment press appeared to be of the same opinion), attributing to them a moral fibre and resilience of spirit which could be far from the truth. I have, I hope, resisted that trap, however, on the basis that "the truth will not appear altogether void of charms, nor ... less pleasing for being within reach of probability", as the enigmatic Peter le Maitre said of his memoirs. In other words, the bare facts already contain sufficient drama to make fanciful elaboration unnecessary.

Hopefully the reader will have been provided with a glimpse of the characters and motives of these historical miscreants to set against the one-sided contemporary pronouncements of judges, magistrates, and newspapermen. It is to be hoped too that the context in which they lived has helped to explain some very human pressures and frailties, and that something of their personalities and motivations can be surmised. Human nature means that there will always be those who break the law, sometimes for reasons that are readily understood. Whatever the true natures of the men and women depicted, it is clear that the gruesome public spectacle of that final leap "into the unfathomable gulph of eternity" is something that should for ever be confined to history books such as this one.

Since 2005, when the first edition of this book was published, Oxford Castle has welcomed tens of thousands of visitors. The experience is certainly no longer like the "continual affrights and terrors" undergone by Anne Green in 1650, and, it is hoped, rather more "somewhat like to Heaven", as Thomas Davis is purported to have found it in 1805. Whatever, it is to be hoped that every visitor and every reader will take just a moment to consider the centuries of human misery imbued in every stone of the original buildings. Whether as diners at a restaurant, or guests at Malmaison Hotel, or customers on a tour, we can think ourselves very fortunate that all we have to do to leave the site is to pay our bill, the modern-day equivalent of the gaoler's fees!

Public executions in Oxford

→>◄←

The table which follows is the most complete list of public executions in Oxford ever published. The principal sources were:

- Anthony Wood's *City of Oxford and Life & Times* for executions held between 1587 and 1688;

- St Thomas' Church parish records from 1697 to 1710;

- The diaries of Thomas Hearne from 1715 to 1730;

- Broadsides and booklets held at the Bodleian Library and online from 1715 to 1752;

- *Jackson's Oxford Journal* from 1754 onwards.

In addition, 25 men and two women are identified in *Oxford Quarter Sessions Order Book 1614–1637*, edited by Robin Blades (2009), as being under sentence of death. Some may have been reprieved, but the following do seem almost certain to have been hanged (probably at Green Ditch) in view of instructions having been specifically given to the city bailiffs in January 1619:

Thomas Sunton alias Joyner (burglary), Samuel Bagnoll, Thomas Kendall, Joan Browne (infanticide), Christopher Lister (burglary), Thomas Andrewes and James Goodwyn (burglaries), and John Frowde ("cutpurse").

All executions from 1650 onwards were certainly hangings – with the exception of Joanna Meads in 1723 (see Appendix 2) – as too, it is assumed, were all prior to that date, albeit the specific evidence is lacking. Two omissions worthy of brief comment occurred as a result of the Civil War:

- Francis Cole was hanged on 7 January 1644 – exceptional as this was a Sunday – being, as Wood's transcript states, "executed for a spie".

- Colonel Francis Windebank was shot on 3 May 1645 on a charge of cowardice. Accounts differ, but this seems to have occurred either in the garden of the castle or somewhere in Broken Hayes (Gloucester Green). The popular tradition that his execution gave rise to the name of "Dead Man's Walk" alongside Merton Field is therefore fallacious.

Key to the table:

(a) = anatomised

(x) = could be fictional

(*) = died a prisoner, but not necessarily executed

  C = executed at Oxford Castle

GD = at Green Ditch

All executions were held above the new main entrance to Oxford Castle in New Road from 1787 onwards. Specified ages are approximate.

Date	Name	Age	Residence/origin	Crime	Site	Notes/source
25 Oct 1587	Harcourt Taverner		Woodeaton	Highway robbery	C	Date buried St Martin's
25 Oct 1587	? Woods (male)		Cumnor		C	Buried St Martin's
1 Mar 1605	Richard Makepeace		Witney		C	Buried St Thomas'
17 July 1607	Leonard de Banke		Minster Lovell		C	Date buried St Thomas'
3 Oct 1609	Robert de Banke (*)		Minster Lovell			Date buried St Thomas'
9 Nov 1610	George Napier (Napper)		Oxford	Treason	C	Hanged, drawn, and quartered
17 July 1612	Thomas de Banke		Minster Lovell		C	Date buried St Thomas'
12 Mar 1618	Richard Busby		Over Norton			Buried St Thomas'
May? 1620	Christopher Wytell				GD?	QS Order Book 1614–1637
May? 1620	William Bushell				GD?	QS Order Book 1614–1637
14 Dec 1650	Anne Green	22	Steeple Barton	Infanticide	C	
10 Aug 1652	Carpenter Carwardyn (Carrodin)			Murder	C	Date buried St Peter-le-Bailey
25 July 1654	? Hussey (male)			Highway robbery	C	Date buried St Peter-le-Bailey
25 July 1654	? Peck (male)			Highway robbery	C	Date buried St Peter-le-Bailey
4 May 1658	Elizabeth Russell?		Oxford	Infanticide	GD	Buried St Mary Magdalen 5 May
15 Mar 1670	Ann Baxter				C	Date buried St Thomas'
17 Mar 1675	William Brewer		Witney		C	Date buried St Thomas'
1 Mar 1676	Richard Harbour		Worcs.		C	Date buried St Thomas'
15 Mar 1680	Thomas Hovell			Murder		Hanged outside Balliol College
4 May 1680	Alice Carpenter		Botley	Infanticide	GD	Wood

Date	Name	Age	Residence/origin	Crime	Site	Notes/source
31 Aug 1681	Stephen Colledge		London	Treason	C	Born Watford, buried London
7 Apr 1688	John Cornet(t)	30		Murder	C	Frenchman
Mar 1692	Mary Goodenough			Infanticide		
20 Mar 1697	William Aldridge					Date buried St Thomas'
20 Mar 1697	John Collett					Date buried St Thomas'
20 Mar 1697	Thomas Minshon					Date buried St Thomas'
30 Mar 1698	John Sones		Oxford			Date buried St Thomas'
19 Aug 1715	Richard Groom		Oxford	Receiving	C	
19 Aug 1715	Mary Emerson (Mrs)			Theft	C	
1716	Jane Sparrow [x]		Oxford	Infanticide		
24 May 1717	? (male)			Burglary	GD	A soldier
24 Mar 1721	? (male) [a]	22	Thame?			Dissected at Exeter College
17 May 1723	Joanna Meads (née Scar(e)brook)	25	Oxford/Combe	Murder of husband	GD	Burned at stake
23 Mar 1724	Jacob Sanders		Reading	Murder	C	Hanged in chains at Caversham
10 Aug 1724	Robert Clarke	17	Wormenhall	Theft	C	Buried St Thomas'
22 Mar 1725	John Protheroe	33	Barton	Murder of wife	C	Born Evesham, 1692
2 Aug 1727	Joan Oliver (Forrester) [a]	40		Murder of child	C	Henley
28 July 1730	William Fuller [a]	26	Caversham	Murder of wife	C	
July 1736?	Jonathan Bradford [x]		Golden Ball Inn	Murder		
27 April 1738	William Clifford?					Journal of John Wesley

Date	Name	Age	Residence/origin	Crime	Site	Notes/source
12? Mar 1749	William Frewin		Oxford	Theft	GD	
12? Mar 1749	Henry Smith		Oxford	Theft	GD	
1 Sept 1749	Paul Wells, gent.	35	Cuddesdon	Forgery	C	Buried Cuddesdon
2 April 1750	James Smith or Wells			Burglary		
2 April 1750	John Walker			Highway robbery		
6 April 1752	Mary Blandy	33	Henley	Patricide	C	Buried Henley
12? Mar 1753	William Grindy			Transportation returnee		Buried St Thomas'
4 Feb 1754	Margaret Dunn (Brown)	30		Theft	GD	
22 Mar 1754	Acton Brice			Highway robbery		
22 Mar 1754	Richard Bayliss			Highway robbery		
26 April 1754	James Till [a]	16/17		Theft		
21 Mar 1755	Richard Mansfield	20		Highway robbery		
21 Mar 1755	Richard Dancer	19		Highway robbery		
28 April 1755	Robert Randall			Sheep-stealing	C	
23 April 1757	John Franklin [a]		Oxford	Murder of wife	GD	
20 Mar 1758	William Hardiman [a]			Highway robbery		
23 Mar 1761	Isaac Darkin (Dumas)	20	London	Highway robbery	C	Buried St Thomas'
22 Mar 1762	Shadrack Smith [a]	59	Charlbury	Theft	C	Born Norwood, Essex
24 July 1762	James Costard [a]		Benson	Matricide		
24 July 1762	Susan Harris [a]		Sydenham	Infanticide		

Date	Name	Age	Residence/origin	Crime	Site	Notes/source
22 April 1765	Parker Hall		Oxford	Theft	C	
10 Mar 1766	Mary Lampry/Lamphrey (Mrs)		Kingham	Murder of grandchild		
28 July 1766	John Milward (Brown)		Northants.	Highway robbery		
28 July 1766	John Williams			Highway robbery		Born Beckley; brother of James (below)
29 Jul 1771	Martin Reader			Burglary (with Cooke)		
16 Aug 1771	William Cooke (Crooke)			Burglary (with Reader)		
23 Mar 1772	Richard Gardner	30	Witney?	Theft		
13 Mar 1775	George Strap [a]	25	Bicester	Murder	C	Born Camsey, Worcs.
14 Aug 1775	James Corbett			Theft		
29 Mar 1776	Richard Churn			Highway robbery	C	
9 Mar 1778	Robert Hitchcock [a]	40	Combe	Patricide		
22 Mar 1779	William Hyde	32	Stanton St John	Theft		Buried Stanton St John
30 Aug 1780	Richard Wells	33	Bampton	Sheep- & horse-theft		Buried Bampton
8 Mar 1784	Daniel Cato [a]		Hook Norton	Murder		
22 Mar 1784	Benjamin Webb (Crawford)	38		Theft		Born Salford, Bath
22 Mar 1784	George Ward (Dagger)	28		Theft		Born Bitton, Glos.
30 Mar 1784	Giles Freeman			Highway robbery		
[7 Mar 1785]	John Price	18	Montgomeryshire	Attempted murder		Hanged in chains, Milton Common
27 Mar 1786	John Cox	31	Henley	Theft and sheep-stealing		Brother of Richard, buried Henley
27 Mar 1786	Richard Cox	21	Henley	Theft and sheep-stealing		Brother of John, buried Henley
27 Mar 1786	John Grace	24		Sheep-stealing		Buried Aston Rowant
27 Mar 1786	Miles Ward	21	London	Theft		Buried London

EXECUTIONS FROM HEREON ALL AT OXFORD CASTLE

Date	Name	Age	Residence/origin	Crime	Notes/source
6 Aug 1787	Thomas White		Woodstock	Theft	Buried St Thomas'
6 Aug 1787	Charles Walter Wyatt	19	Witney	Embezzlement	
24 Mar 1788	Charles Smith	28		Horse-theft	
22 Mar 1790	Thomas Smith (Davis)		London	Horse-theft	
19 July 1790	John Castle [a]	31/35	Abingdon	Murder	
19 July 1790	Charles Evans Shury [a]	42	Abingdon	Murder	
2 Aug 1790	James Williams	30/34		Horse-theft	Born Beckley; brother of John (above)
7 Mar 1791	Giles Freeman Covington [a]	23	Abingdon	Murder	Skeleton retained for lectures
21 Mar 1791	John Davis (Kelly)	27		Highway robbery	Born Carmarthenshire
26 Mar 1792	Joseph Tapp	29		Highway robbery	
29 July 1793	Robert Jenkinson			Horse-theft	
21 Aug 1797	John Marshall	32		Horse-theft	Born Durham
21 Aug 1797	Thomas Andrews	37/39	Oxford	Horse-theft	Born Daylesford, Glos.
21 Aug 1797	William Use	24		Burglary	Born Manchester
26 Mar 1798	James Carpenter	23/24		Burglary	Born East Sheen, London
28 July 1800	Edward Thorn	59		Murder	Born Steventon
23 Mar 1801	Jesse Wiggins	45	Henley	Sheep-stealing	Buried Castle
25 Mar 1805	Thomas Davis	43		Counterfeiting	Born Droitwich; buried Castle
10 July 1815	James Banister [a]	45	Shillingford	Murder of wife	
24 Mar 1817	William Archer	59	Great Bourton?	Arson	Born & buried Mollington

Date	Name	Age	Residence/origin	Crime	Notes/source
3 Aug 1818	John Bradley	23	Bicester?	Highway robbery	Born Bicester
3 Aug 1818	Richard Wiggins	26	Waterperry	Sheep-stealing	Born Piddington; buried St Thomas'
5 Aug 1822	John Matthews	30		Highway robbery	Born Wilts., buried Castle
2 Aug 1824	William James [a]	40/48	Taynton	Murder	Born Burford
2 Aug 1824	Henry Pittaway [a]	25	Swinbrook	Murder	Born Swinbrook
20 Mar 1826	William Clack	21/22	Great Milton	Horse-theft	Born Black Bourton; buried Castle
26 Mar 1827	Richard Webb	39	Cookham Dean	Horse-theft	Born Mapledurham, buried Castle
13 Aug 1827	George Allum			Murder	
24 Mar 1828	Thomas Shaylor	22	Bampton?	Highway robbery	Born & buried Standlake
19 Mar 1832	John (or George) Gibbs	32	Steeple Aston	Arson	Buried Castle
19 Mar 1832	George Lay	18/19	Abingdon?	Attempted murder	Buried Culham
5 Mar 1836	Thomas Clay	25	Elsfield or Headington	Murder	Buried Castle
23 Mar 1840	Charles Morley	34	Woodcote	Murder	Buried Castle
22 Mar 1852	William Kalabergo	22	Banbury	Murder	Buried Castle
24 Mar 1863	Noah Austin	26	Upper Heyford	Murder	Buried Castle

APPENDIX 2

Green Ditch

→>◄←

The city execution site at Green Ditch was next to the one-mile stone on the Banbury Road. The ditch itself was about four feet wide and three deep, marking the northern extent of the old Oxford city boundary, along the line of today's St Margaret's Road. It appears to have been used as a place of execution from at least 1285, according to an implied occurrence recounted in Margaret Gelling's *Place Names of Oxfordshire*. In that year, a condemned man was rescued from near St Giles' Church while en route to the gallows – a forerunner of the challenges that the authorities faced in preventing public interference in later centuries. By the late-eighteenth and early-nineteenth centuries it was also known as "Gallows Baulk".*

The earliest known specific reference to "Grene Diche" dates from 1318, in the Register of Godstow Nunnery, and in 1375, when the structure was overturned by members of the University, Green Ditch was distinguished as the location of the gallows erected specifically under the authority of the Oxford burgesses. Several accounts of the executions in January 1400 of more than twenty of

---

* Green Ditch also served a less morbid civic purpose, as the place where visitors of especially high rank would be met by the mayor to be escorted into the city. Queen Elizabeth I was greeted in this way in 1566, James I in 1603, and Charles II in 1663.

the principal instigators of a plot to overthrow Henry IV suggest that they occurred at Green Ditch. This seems difficult to substantiate, in the light of a translation of a contemporary manuscript – *Chronicque de la Traïson et Mort de Richart Deux Roy dEngleterre* (Benjamin Williams, 1846) – in which Sir Thomas Blount and Sir Benet or Benedict Sely or Shelley are described as being "drawn from Oxford unto the place of execution, a long league or more". A league is an imprecise unit of measurement, although in England it is usually about three miles, so much farther away than Green Ditch – although it is quite possible that the distance mentioned included a preliminary parade of the condemned men around the city. Blount was subsequently subjected to a gruesome hanging, evisceration, beheading, and quartering. The same text asserts that approximately 27 other rebels, including Thomas Wintershull, John Walsh, and Baldwin of Kent, were beheaded at Oxford Castle itself.

The cost of erecting an "execution tree" at Green Ditch appears in the council chamberlain's accounts for 1616/17, and again in the years 1629/30, 1634/35, and 1657/58. The latter cost of £1 12s 6d was "for making a pair of gallows and setting of them up at Green Ditch and for cutting down a tree and bring it home" [sic]. If one reads this to mean that one set of gallows was left standing, it must have been those used for the failed hanging on 4 May 1658 of Elizabeth Russell, Mrs Cope's maid, described in Chapter 6.

Other people known to have been executed at Green Ditch are Alice Carpenter of Botley on 4 May 1680, for killing her illegitimate child; an unnamed soldier whose hanging on Friday 24 May 1717 was noted by Thomas Hearne; and Joanna Meads, the only known case of immolation, this being the specific penalty for the murder of a husband, on 17 May 1723. The source for the background to this case is Thomas Hearne, who described Robert Meads, her husband, as "a very honest, industrious brewer" in St Ebbe's parish. His wife had been baptised as Joane Scarisbrook at Combe, near Woodstock, in January 1697, and the pair had married in Oxford in 1718. According to Hearne, (calling her "Hannah") Joanna was a "young, brisk, tight woman ... a great company keeper and notorious for her lascivious loose life", and her father, [John] Scaresbrook, was "a great rogue". Meads' death had occurred the day after he had consumed an apple dumpling cooked and served to him by his wife, "being without doubt poysoned".* She was held at the city prison, the Bocardo, but, with a suggestion of connivance by the keeper of the prison, escaped the following month. Disguised as a man, she got as far as London, but was arrested at Wapping on the very day that she had arranged to board a foreign-bound ship. The execution took place at Green Ditch. Hearne noted on 23 May that "she was first strangled and then burnt to ashes" and that the charred stump still remained "just on the right hand of the road leading to Bicester, whereas they us'd to be executed on the left hand just in the ditch".

Only four further Green Ditch executions are known: two young thieves, "much lamented by the inhabitants, being their first offence", in 1749, and a female thief five years later. *Jackson's* report on the execution of Margaret Dunn on Monday 4 February 1754 stated that the gallows had been "erected for that purpose", indicating that the structure was not permanent, but perhaps implying by this very mention that it had been so in the past. Dunn had been arrested for a theft committed three years earlier, but had escaped and remained at liberty until only a month or so before her execution. Behaving "with amazing intrepidity", she "spoke near half an hour at the

---

* He was buried St Ebbe's on 10 November 1722.

place of execution, and confessed herself to have been involved in all kinds of wickedness except murder, to which detestable crime she professed the utmost abhorrence". Of all the people executed at Oxford in the eighteenth century, Dunn is the only one whose religious belief is specified, namely Roman Catholicism. She was sufficiently notorious, under the alias of "the famous Mary Brown", for at least two London newspapers to remark on the hanging. In those accounts, she was described as "a well-looking woman, about thirty years of age", and was reported to have voiced the not unreasonable opinion that she thought her crime "too small an offence to lose her life for".

There was no such dispute at the last execution known to have been held at Green Ditch, on Saturday 23 April 1757, because John Franklin was a self-confessed murderer. The victim had been his own pregnant wife, and Franklin's body was claimed by the anatomists without resistance. *Jackson's* called him a member of "a gang who lurk about and infest the country, cloaking their villainies under pretence of getting a livelihood by horsetaking" (where men would endeavour to retrieve stolen horses in order to claim a reward, much as "thief-takers" did; it was a less-than-respected profession, often used as a cover for actual horse theft). With misguided optimism, Franklin was known beforehand to have entertained bets of two and three to one that he would be acquitted. And there must indeed have been some possibility of that, since the trial lasted five hours. Unusually, the time of Franklin's execution was late in the day, *Jackson's* observing that he was "put in the cart about four o'clock in the afternoon wherein he stood upright and read very loud and distinct all the way to Green Ditch". At the gallows he "continued reading and praying aloud without the least hesitation for an hour with amazing spirits". Then "the cart drew away …".

Although John Franklin is the last person known to have been executed at Green Ditch, it appears that the practice might have continued for a further 20 years or so, since Sir John Peshall, writing in 1773 (in *The Antient and Present State of the City of Oxford*), referred to "Greenditch, or Woditch, where the city gallows stood, but now are occasionally placed". Between 1757 and 1787 there were some 20 Oxford executions where no location was specified, but thereafter it is certain that Green Ditch no longer hosted such occasions, in view of the unfailing use of the gateway to the newly rebuilt prison from 1787 onwards (see Chapter 8).

Jack Ketch and
others of his deadly trade

→>-<+

Almost all the executions that occurred in Oxford during the period covered by this book were very public in nature, yet in all that time that key agent in the gruesome dance of death, the executioner, was identified on only one occasion. As it happens, the man in question that day in 1681 was England's most famous hangman of all time. This was Jack Ketch, also known as John Catch (and ironically as "Squire Ketch") of London, who was probably appointed in 1663 and became famous as the presiding figure of the executions which were held at Tyburn eight times a year. His notorious blend of brutality and incompetence established the generic use of his name for centuries after his own death.

The execution that warranted bringing Ketch to Oxford was unusual in the Oxford context for being conducted on a charge of treason. His victim that day, a carpenter called Stephen Colledge (c.1635–1681), had been found guilty of advocating resistance to Charles II in March 1681, as the king was making his way from Oxford back to London. After his arrest, Colledge, dubbed "the Protestant joiner", was taken to the Tower of London in June. His case was dismissed the following month, but not to the satisfaction of his accusers. Additional evidence was gathered, and a second trial arranged in Oxford, where it was felt that a jury might more readily comply with the wishes of the Crown. It did, despite widespread misgivings among the public, finding that Colledge had "prepared arms, armed himself, and incited and advised ... others to ... seize the person of the king at Oxford". The trial took all day and a verdict was not reached until the early hours of the following morning. The sentence (as recorded in one of several contemporary commentaries on the case, *The Tryal of Stephen Colledge*) was:

> You shall be drawn on a hurdle to the place of execution, where you shall be hanged up by the neck, and be cut down alive, your privy members shall be cut off, and your bowels taken out and burnt before your face, your hand shall be cut off from your body, your body be divided into four quarters, which are to be at the king's dispose.

Colledge's response to hearing this cheering news was a simple "Amen". On the fatal day, Wednesday 31 August 1681, he was executed against the gate of the castle. After embracing his son, and "kissing him several times with great passion", Colledge made a long speech, the contents of which can be summarised in one sentence, recorded in *The Dying Words of Stephen Colledge* (printed by his own relations) as: "I am reported to be a papist, I declare I was bred a protestant, such have I lived, and such I die."

And the man who made sure that he died was Jack Ketch, named in *The Speech and Carriage of Stephen Colledge at Oxford*, which concludes with: "The executioner, Ketch, desired his pardon, and he said, I do forgive you. The Lord have mercy on my soul." The only concession to Colledge's gruesome sentence was that he was spared posthumous public display. The *Dying Words* broadside concludes: "About the 12 of the clock at noon he was executed and his head and quarters (through his Majesty's grace) delivered to his relations, and by them brought up to London, to be privately interred."*

Ketch went on to terminate the lives of such high profile individuals as Lord William Russell in 1683 (which he badly bungled, being obliged to issue a public apology afterwards) and the Duke of Monmouth (Charles II's illegitimate son) in 1685, which occasion sealed Ketch's reputation for ineptitude. He died in November 1686. His wife had remained loyal in the face of almost universal execration, if the dramatist John Dryden is a reliable guide. In "Progress of Satire" (within *Select Essays on the Belles Lettres*, 1750) are the lines: "A man may be capable, as Jack Ketch's wife said of his servant, of a plain piece of work, a bare hanging, but to make a malefactor die sweetly was only belonging to her husband."

After his death, Ketch's notoriety was such that his name became a generic term for an executioner. James Woodforde used the term in his own eye-witness account of the execution of George Strap in 1775 (see Chapter 6), and *Jackson's Oxford Journal* considered that its readers would be familiar with the allusion when reporting the execution of Robert Jenkinson in 1793: "He had been fervent in prayer previous to his being brought out, but was totally silent at the place of execution, and the moment Jack Ketch had fixed the halter the drop took place." Another example comes in Dickens' *Oliver Twist* (1837–39). Fagin and Nancy are talking about Bill Sikes, and the inevitability of his arrest, when the former tells her to "murder him yourself, if you would have him escape Jack Ketch".

---

* George Napier (or Napper), who resided in Holywell Manor, a Catholic "safe house", was shown no such leniency after his own similar death in 1610. According to Anthony Wood, he was "hanged, drawn and quartered in the castle yard. The next day his head and quarters were set upon the 4 gates of the city, and upon that great one belonging to Christ Church … to the great terror of the Catholics".

When outlining the story of Anne Green, G. V. Cox (*Recollections*, 1870) selected this example as one of many subsequent "attempts at wit":

> Ann Green was a slippery quean,
> In vain did the jury detect her: –
> She cheated Jack Ketch, and then the vile wretch
> 'Scap'd the knife of the learned dissector.

The longevity of Ketch's name comes largely as a result of the contemporary appearance in England of the Punch and Judy puppet show.* Introduced from Italy, the anglicised version of the name Pulcinella – Punch – had been adopted by the 1680s, when Ketch was at the height of his fame. Punch is an unashamedly violent character, yet he is also the hero of the piece, as a free-spirited individual attempting to resist the constraints of family, religion, and state. It is his resistance to the latter which Punch exhibits when he outwits the hangman, who inevitably became equated with the infamous Ketch in the popular mind. Punch, facing the gallows for (in most versions) killing his wife Judy, pretends not to understand how to put his head through the noose. The gullible Ketch eventually demonstrates the technique himself, at which point Punch kicks away the ladder. This scene is described by "Bernard Blackmantle" in *The English Spy* (1826) as "the *ne plus ultra* of his comicalities … Mr. John Ketch hangs suspended in the air – Punch shouts a glorious triumph – all the world backs him in his conquest". It mirrors the sentiment of many executions, where the criminal was frequently seen as a victimised hero, while the hangman, the agent of state oppression, was the villain.

---

* See, for example, *The Punch and Judy Show* by Robert Leach (1985).

Other than Ketch, the names of only two Oxford executioners are known before 1852, when England's most famous executioner of the nineteenth century, William Calcraft, officiated (as he did too for the last of all public executions in Oxford, that of Noah Austin in 1863). Both men's names are revealed not as a result of contemporary reporting of their role but as retrospective asides. With largely baffling use of italics, *Jackson's* of 26 April 1760 reflected the inevitability of continued lawlessness in reporting that the former hangman James Crozier had enlisted in the army. Crozier,

> who in the *execution* of that office, has *put to death* many magnanimous *heroes*, inlisted himself into one of the new in-*dependent* companies. Probably at the end of the war, when his services *abroad* shall become unnecessary, he may at *home* find sufficient employment in his old profession.

The other identifiable Oxford hangman was William Blackhall. When he was committed to the castle charged with stealing "the carcass of a dead fat hog" in Henley in March 1787, *Jackson's* noted that he had "on a former occasion officiated as hangman". It may be that he had done so while imprisoned on a previous charge. Prisoners certainly did undertake the role – at the executions of Anne Green in 1650 (William Petty, in *The Petty Papers*, appears to identify him as "old Townesend") and Thomas Davis in 1805, for instance. As too, probably, the light-fingered individual who executed Richard Gardner (for numerous robberies and burglaries in Witney) on Monday 23 March 1772. The reward given to any prisoner who undertook the role is never overtly specified, but it may be that after this episode the treat of a good night's rest in the gaoler's own house may well have been reconsidered.

Jackson's of 28 March 1772 observed:

> The fellow who officiated as hangman, being lodged the preceding
> night in one of the rooms of the dwelling house belonging to the
> keeper, was so little affected by Gardner's approaching catastrophe
> that he stole a pair of plated buckles and two handkerchiefs, but
> finding himself suspected, he threw down the handkerchiefs and
> pretended innocence.

This is as clear an example as any of the impotence of capital
punishment! If the authorities intended the sight of a felon expiring
in torments of terror and agony to be a frightful warning to those
who watched, they were mistaken. If the lesson was not heeded by
the hangman, that most intimate witness of those last horrifying
moments of ebbing life, then, one has to ask, who *was* likely to
heed it? The whole capital punishment debate is neatly summarised
in this exchange between Punch and Ketch from an early printed
script: when Ketch asks him, "Why were you so cruel as to commit
so many murders?" Punch responds, "But that's no reason why you
should be cruel too, and murder me."

APPENDIX 4
Anatomical studies in Oxford

→>-<+

However antisocial their activities while alive, some of those individuals who were executed at Oxford did at least make posthumous amends with unwitting (and almost always unwilling) contributions to anatomical understanding.

The first Oxford University Reader in Anatomy was appointed in 1624. This was Thomas Clayton (1575–1647), first Master of Pembroke College, for whom the task of acquiring after every Lent assizes "a Sounde body of one of the Executed persons" was of especial importance, since a pre-existing University statute required that undergraduates had to witness at least two dissections in order to gain a medical degree. They also had to be supervised in undertaking two anatomisations themselves before they could practise as surgeons in their own right. The Reader was also required afterwards to arrange a "decent burial of the body and all the necessaries thereunto".

Despite this authorisation, the reluctance of friends and relatives of the deceased to part with the corpse was an ongoing cause of confrontation. To address the issue, a charter was issued by Charles I in 1636 which permitted the Reader of Anatomy to demand the body of any person executed within 21 miles of Oxford. It was a measure which nonetheless continued to meet with great resistance, such that in August 1710 a German visitor, Conrad von Uffenbach, observed that anatomical lectures "scarcely ever happen". Even the one that had been scheduled at the time was cancelled, because "there was no corpse, the doctor having failed to get one from London". The Quaker John Bellers shows why Oxford doctors were required to look farther afield. In his 1714 *Essay towards the Improvement of Physick,* he wrote: "At present its not easie for the students to get a body to dissect at Oxford, the mob are so mutinous to prevent their having one."

Unsurprisingly perhaps, given this mismatch between expiring criminals and aspiring doctors, desperate measures were sometimes adopted. Body-snatching was not as common in Oxford as in some larger cities, but the diarist Thomas Hearne did note in 1724 that the wife of Jacob Richards had been buried inside St Peter-in-the-East church rather than in the graveyard "to prevent her being taken up again, it being common practise nowadays for young physicians to rob church yards". Furthermore, it was "young people, especially young women, that they generally seek". This led Hearne to recall one macabrely amusing incident when "a pretty young woman" was buried in the same churchyard: a "search was made in the night time for her body, but they mistook her grave and took up one Goody Beecham, an old woman who had been bedmaker of Edmund Hall and was buried at the same time". Being disturbed, however, the culprits abandoned their exanimate cargo, leaving her "bolt upright, just under Edmund Hall against the wall, where (before day) … she, being seen, frightened some people, who knew nothing about the matter".*

---

* The register of St Peter-in-the-East shows: Katharine Willis (spinster) buried on 14 January 1704; Elizabeth Beacham (widow) buried on 16 January 1704.

Hearne became inevitably acquainted with the topic of anatomisation on account of his position as Assistant Keeper of the Bodleian Library, because the University's Anatomy School occupied the first floor of the south side of what is now the Old Bodleian Library, facing Radcliffe Square. It would seem that individual colleges occasionally arranged additional impromptu dissections. Hearne noted that after the hanging of an unnamed young man on 14 March 1721, "the scholars, having combin'd to have him dissected, took the body away by force, abused the father and mother ... & carried the body off naked, upon their shoulders, to Exeter College, where one Dr Furneux of that college dissected it". A decade later, after the "desperate riot" which ensued after the execution of the murderer William Fuller (see Chapter 6), his corpse was eventually dissected at Christ Church.

The Murder Act of 1751/52 was an attempt both to improve the supply of corpses for medical research and "for better preventing the horrid crime of murder ... that some further terror and peculiar mark of infamy be added to the punishment". The Act ordered that the corpses of murderers could, if the judge specified, be left suspended in chains in full view, as an example to others who might be tempted down the same path. No funeral was allowed to take place until after the dissection. The Act also specified that the execution should take place the next day but one following sentence, unless that should be a Sunday. With the Oxford assizes normally ending on a Friday, the majority of executions described in this book therefore took place on a Monday.

While this statute clarified the situation regarding murderers, the University maintained that the 1636 charter also sustained its legal right to the corpses of other executed persons too. This led inevitably to many more unsavoury post-execution corporeal tugs-of-war. The violence which followed the executions of Acton Brice and Richard Bayliss in 1754 (when the London *Public Advertiser* noted that the "Professor of Physick" had specifically invoked the charter) is a case in point; as too with Robert Randall in 1755 and Isaac Darkin in 1761.

In the case of actual murderers, however, there appears to have been little public protest. The first to be convicted in Oxford after the passing of the Murder Act was John Franklin, in 1757 (see Appendix 2), after which his body was sent to the "Museum", that is the Old Ashmolean in Broad Street (now the University Museum of the History of Science), where the University's chemistry laboratory doubled as a venue for anatomical lectures. William Hardiman's

FIGURE 24 The Christ Church Anatomy School, from James Ingram's 1837 *Memorials of Oxford*.

body was taken to the same venue the next year, followed by Shadrack Smith, James Costard, and Susan Harris, all in 1762.

Later in that century Christ Church became the official venue for anatomical lectures, with the creation of a new, purpose-built Anatomy School. It was founded using the bequest of a college alumnus, Dr Matthew Lee, who died in 1755, although it took until 1767 for the building to be completed. It is presumed that from then on all dissections took place at Christ Church, although no specific records survive. George Strap, in March 1775, was the first individual known to have been delivered to Christ Church, followed by Robert Hitchcock in 1778 (see Chapter 6); Daniel Cato in 1784; Charles Evans Shury and John Castle in 1790; and Giles Freeman Covington in 1791 (see Chapter 7). Given the continuing widespread resentment and suspicion of the general populace, Christ Church was surreptitious about its new facility – "Skeleton Corner" as it was dubbed – and it was positioned so that "the bodies could be brought to the school by a back entrance, without scandal to the College."*

The Murder Act was amended in 1832 by the Anatomy Act, under which it was possible for the University to acquire unclaimed bodies from workhouses and hospitals. Although the corpse of an executed criminal could still be hung in chains, automatic dissection was discontinued, and from then on even men executed for murder could be buried within the precincts of the prison. The first such was Thomas Clay in 1836, although men executed for lesser crimes had been buried at the prison from 1801 onwards.

---

* "Skeleton Corner" was a term in use since at least the 1790s, viz. a letter of 15 April 1812 from Robert Southey to his Christ Church contemporary, Charles Wynn: "It is now eighteen years since you and I used to sit till midnight over your claret in Skeleton Corner."

Oxford Archaeology made a thorough survey of Oxford Castle before it was reopened in 2005. A total of 73 articulated skeletons were discovered, and of the 62 that date from the post-Medieval period, 34 could be identified as probably or possibly male and nine as probably or possibly female. Only five show definite signs of anatomisation, although, as Oxford Archaeology's report on the work undertaken between 1999 and 2008 states, "modifications like these can be difficult to interpret ... because they may be the result of several different activities including in vivo surgery autopsy or dissection".

FIGURE 25 The *Jackson's Oxford Journal* masthead for its second issue of 12 May 1753. The newspaper consisted of four pages throughout the century, with only a very small proportion devoted to local news. The newspaper seems faithfully to have recorded every execution held in the city, and is often the sole source for identifying the fate of the corpse.

APPENDIX 5

William Jackson (1721–1795), founder of *Jackson's Oxford Journal*

-﹥-﹤-

Despite his enormous influence on Oxford affairs, and the primary source material that his weekly newspaper has provided for countless Oxford local historians since its first issue in May 1753, very little is known about William Jackson himself. Although he printed millions of words about other people, his own life was apparently so mundane that virtually nothing was written about him either during his lifetime or afterwards. His newspaper's contribution to the understanding of historical criminality and punishment (as well as of almost every other aspect of daily life) is so important, however, that a short biographical sketch is long overdue.*

When William Jackson died on 22 April 1795, the obituary in the newspaper that carried his name, *Jackson's Oxford Journal*, was strangely subdued:

> Died on Wednesday morning last, aged upwards of seventy, William Jackson, Esq. proprietor & publisher of this journal ever since its first establishment. In his publick characterisation his loss

---

* A version of this account, the first to appear in any book, was published in the *Oxford Times* "Limited Edition" magazine of November 2009. Since then, additional biographical information was communicated to me (mainly in September 2012) by Derrick Holt, a descendant of William Jackson's sister, Rachel.

will be long felt. In private life he was warm in his attachments, and sincere in his friendships.

As its founder, one might have expected his own newspaper to have marked Jackson's passing with words of a more fulsome and heartfelt nature. The brevity of the item seems to tell a tale of its own: for all the influence and wealth that he accumulated in a publishing career spanning five decades, and for all the exposure that his pages gave to countless thousands of other people, Jackson himself appears never to have revealed even a glimpse of his own private life, nor apparently cultivated much affection.

He never married or had children, there are no known images of him, and it is only now that his origins – his birth was registered at the Quaker meeting house in Bradford on 7 March 1721 – can be stated. His parents, William Jackson and Sarah North, had at least seven children, his older sister Rachel (1707–1775) being the only one known to have had any children of her own, after marrying James Lister (1710–1753), also at the Bradford Quaker meeting house, in 1734. Significantly, Lister was a printer and also a proprietor of the *Leeds Mercury*, and this seems likely to have influenced his brother-in-law William Jackson in his own choice of career.*

It is not known exactly when or why William Jackson came to Oxford, although it is probable that he did so with the specific intention of launching a newspaper. The first issue of his *Oxford Flying Weekly Journal & Cirencester Gazette* appeared in September 1746. His partner in the venture, Robert Walker, was already well established in the London and provincial newspaper trade. Indeed,

---

* Jackson's nephew James Lister married Elizabeth Franklin in Oxford in 1764. One of their sons, William (?–1843), married in 1791 Elizabeth Early (c.1769–1847?), from the famous Witney blanket-manufacturing family, which also had early Quaker affiliations.

one of Walker's titles was the *Cambridge Journal*, launched in 1744, which should have given him an unmatched ability to assess the potential afforded by the sister city. However, it would seem that they had both underestimated the difficulty of setting up in competition with the long-standing *Oxford Gazette & Reading Mercury*, even if it was printed in Reading rather than Oxford. As a consequence, Jackson's first newspaper venture lasted fewer than three years, with the last issue of the *Gazette* appearing in June 1749.

Jackson then concentrated on books, printing many over the next few years on various subjects.* Displaying both pragmatism and humility, he also acted as an Oxford agent for his erstwhile rival, the *Mercury*, until June 1755.†

Much the wiser, no doubt, after a lull of nearly four years Jackson saw another opportunity to launch a newspaper. The very long prelude to the Oxfordshire parliamentary election of 1754 was notoriously violent, expensive, and vituperative. The first local election for more than forty years, the result had national implications of immense significance. It was less than a decade since Bonnie Prince Charlie's unsuccessful attempt to restore the House of Stuart to the English throne. Oxfordshire's elite remained notably sympathetic to his cause, with the result that the election distilled into a battle between the "Old Interest" Jacobite Tories versus the "New Interest" Whigs, who supported the incumbent House of Hanover in the personification of King George II.

---

* This included *A genuine and impartial account*, one of the many accounts of the life and trial of Mary Blandy, which he printed in collaboration with Robert Walker in London in 1752.
† A fellow agent was the father of the future pioneer of hot-air ballooning, the Oxford pastry-cook James Sadler (see my biography *'King of all Balloons'*, published in 2015). Without *Jackson's* account of his first flight on 4 October 1784, this momentous moment of aviation history would have passed unrecorded.

In April 1753, first one side, then the other, produced a highly biased handbill, full of derogatory contradictions. William Jackson saw the need for a neutral voice, and the first issue of *Jackson's Oxford Journal* appeared on 5 May 1753. Somehow, although overtly Tory in his personal outlook, Jackson managed to maintain sufficient neutrality to ensure that the newspaper survived and flourished. He was confident enough to stake his reputation on it, quite literally, by including his name in the title. He was not unique among eighteenth-century newspaper proprietors in being either bold or vain enough to proclaim such a clear personal association, but he was unusual. This time, leaving the Reading-based *Gazette* to concentrate more on Berkshire affairs, his newspaper went from strength to strength.

Producing and selling newspapers was only one of William Jackson's business interests, however. From his first arrival in Oxford, he also retailed numerous patent medicines, ointments, and other quack remedies which purported to cure everything from leprosy and rickets to hypochondriac melancholy and sterility. These and other items, including many printed works and books, could be purchased from Jackson's offices and press in the High Street.

In 1768, Jackson's already considerable business interests received a huge fillip when he was authorised by the University to commission and print the Oxford Almanacs, which he continued to do until 1788, by which time the University had also (in 1780) awarded Jackson the distinctive and lucrative right to print bibles. In 1782 he exerted control over the supply side of his business by leasing and modernising the Duke of Marlborough's paper mill at Wolvercote, which he ran until 1793.

Ever since the opening of Oxford's new Covered Market in 1774, Jackson's business premises had formed part of its façade, occupying

Nos. 10 to 12 High Street. At No. 15, in one of the new retail outlets adjacent to the famous and ancient Mitre Inn, was a fishmonger's shop known as "Mrs Jones's". It had been run since the death of their mother, Elizabeth Jones, in 1773 by her four unmarried daughters (their father Thomas having died in 1747). Their younger sister Mary (1741–1815) found work in Jackson's printing office, and evidently earned the particular esteem of her employer – and much else besides! – because, on his death in 1795, she was left the bulk of his estate. And very considerable it was, most substantially his country mansion, Headington House, which had been completed in 1783.

The inheritance entitled the unmarried fishmonger's daughter to call herself Lady Heddington (not to be confused with the separate Manor of Headington), Jackson having acquired the title in 1786, the same year that he was made an honorary freeman of the city. But that was not all! She also inherited Jackson's farm at Barton and soon found herself in possession of the *Journal's* premises in the High Street too, as they were immediately transferred to her by Jackson's only surviving sister, Sarah Grimshaw (1716–1804).

Sarah Grimshaw also swiftly disposed of her brother's many other properties. Within a total of 14 lots advertised for auction in *Jackson's* of 4 July and 11 July 1795 were two large houses in New Inn Hall Lane. These were purchased by the Oxford Canal Company, which subsequently resold one of them to the Oxford gaoler Daniel Harris (see Chapter 2).*

Quite why William Jackson showed such great generosity to Mary Jones is unknown. The act sheds the only glimmer of light

---

* William Jackson had been a proprietor of the Oxford Canal Company, attending board meetings in Oxford since at least 1791; two other lots auctioned by his sister were ten original canal shares and six bonds, worth in total more than £2,000.

on the domestic life of this secretive, life-long bachelor, for whom, it would seem, business was his only passion. Considering his enormous importance for both the townspeople of Oxford and the University, for both Town and Gown, Jackson's passing attracted very little attention, and one gets the impression that he was respected rather than liked. A cryptic footnote in John Nichols' *Literary Anecdotes of the Eighteenth Century* was a rare acknowledgment of "a man of no extraordinary abilities, but one who dared", and whose newspaper was "the only sterling, political, electioneering, controversy that ever existed – where, not parties only, but private persons from the throne to the mechanic" gained exposure. It is this, William Jackson's revelations about the activities of so many ordinary, and yet extraordinary, Oxfordshire individuals, for which all local and family historians will be forever grateful.*

* *Jackson's Oxford Journal* remained as Oxford's only newspaper until 1806. In 1899 it was bought by the Oxford Times Company and its last issue appeared in 1909, after which it was renamed the *Oxford Journal Illustrated*.

Sources and further reading

→>-<←

BLADES, ROBIN (ed.)   *Oxford Quarter Sessions Order Book 1614–1637,* 2009

BOARDMAN, CARL   *Oxfordshire Sinners and Villains,* 1994

Foul Deeds and Suspicious Deaths around Oxfordshire, 2004

BRINDLEY, GILES   *Oxford Crime, Death & Debauchery,* 2009

COLDHAM, PETER WILSON   *Bonded Passengers for America* (vol. 6 for the Oxford circuit), 1983

The Complete Book of Emigrants in Bondage 1614–1775, 1988

King's Passengers to Maryland and Virginia, 1997

[COOKE, J. (printer)]   *Cries of Blood, or Juryman's Monitor,* 1767

COX, G.V.   *Recollections of Oxford* (2nd edition), 1870

DAVENPORT, J.M.   *Notes as to Oxford Castle,* 1877

DAVIES, MARK   *Stories of Oxford Castle,* 2006

The Abingdon Waterturnpike Murder, 2008

DAVIES, MARK & ROBINSON, CATHERINE   *A Towpath Walk in Oxford,* 2012

DAVIES, MARK   *'King of all Balloons',* 2017

ELRINGTON, C.R. (ed.)   *Victoria History of the County of Oxford,* 1979

GOVE, PHILIP BABCOCK   "An Oxford Convict in Maryland" from *The Maryland Historical Review* (June 1942)

GRETTON, MARY STURGE	*Oxfordshire Justices of the Peace in the Seventeenth Century*, 1934
HEARNE, THOMAS	*Remarks and Collections*, 1885–1921
HIBBERT, C. & E. (eds.)	*Encyclopaedia of Oxford*, 1988
HOOPER, MARY	*Newes from the Dead*, 2008
HOWARD, JOHN	*The State of the Prisons in England and Wales etc.* 1777, 1780, & 1782 (1st, 2nd & 3rd editions)
	The State of the Prisons in England and Wales etc. 1792 (4th edition)
	Appendix to The State of the Prisons in England and Wales etc., 1784
	An Account of the Principal Lazarettos of Europe etc, 1789
KING, EDWARD	*Vestiges of Oxford Castle*, 1796
MORGAN, JOAN	*Mary Blandy*, 1979, first published as *The Hanging Tree*, 1950
NEILD, JAMES	*Account of the … Society for the Discharge and Relief of Persons Imprisoned for Small Debts*, 1800 & 1808
	State of the Prisons in England, Scotland, and Wales, 1812
OXFORD ARCHAEOLOGY	*Castle, Canal & College* (historic context study and conservation plan), 2008
PESHALL, JOHN	*History of the University of Oxford*, 1773
PITT, MOSES	*The Cry of the Oppressed*, 1691
PLOT, ROBERT	*The Natural History of Oxford-shire*, 1677
PRIOR, MARY	*Fisher Row*, 1982
REIMES, PHILIP DE	*The Romance of Blonde of Oxford*, (ed. M le Roux de Lincy), 1858
RICHMOND, CAROL	*Banished!* 2007
SINCLAIR, H.M. & ROBB-SMITH, A.H.T.	*A Short History of Anatomical Teaching in Oxford*, 1950

SQUIRES, THOMAS   *In West Oxford*, 1928

THACKER, FRED   *The Thames Highway*, 1968 (reprints of 1914 & 1920)

THOMPSON, J.M.   "The Robbery from the Ashmolean Museum,
                  1776" and "Le Maitre, alias Marat" in *English
                  Historical Review*, Jan. 1931 & Jan. 1934

WESLEY, JOHN   *Journals*, 1909–1916

WOOD, ANTHONY   *Life & Times*, 1891–1900

WOODFORDE JAMES   *Diary of a Country Parson 1785–1802*, 1953

Index

✦➤◄✦

Index of main names and places (excluding Appendix 1; Oxford, London and counties).

Places are in present-day Oxfordshire, and churches/parishes in Oxford, unless otherwise stated. For Oxford public houses, colleges, and streets see under "Oxford"; for ships and hulks see under "Ships". Places in **bold** appear in Figure 1 (pages x and xi).

ALICE in WATERLAND
Mark J. Davies

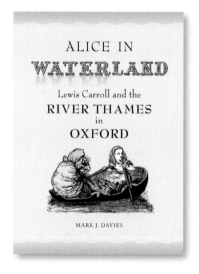

A virtual cruise along the River Thames, highlighting the people, places, and events which inspired the world's most famous children's story.

'A lovely book; simultaneously scholarly and fun.' *Oxford Times*

'Packed with lively and enthusiastic speculation.' *Times Literary Supplement*

'Full of enthralling information … intelligent and comprehensive.' *Lewis Carroll Society*

'A splendid book – fully informative and marvellously detailed; a really important addition to the literature of Lewis Carroll and Oxford.' *Philip Pullman*

'Brings the locations of the stories vividly to life.' Edward Wakeling, editor of *Lewis Carroll's Diaries*

ISBN 978-1-908493-69-9

Published jointly by
Oxford Towpath Press www.oxfordwaterwalks.co.uk
and Signal Books www.signalbooks.co.uk

 For the author's range of guided walks, see **www.oxfordwaterwalks.co.uk**

A TOWPATH WALK IN OXFORD

The Canal and River Thames between Wolvercote and the City

MARK DAVIES AND CATHERINE ROBINSON

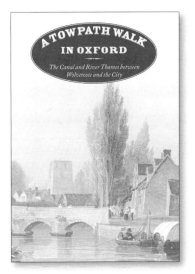

A *Towpath Walk in Oxford* takes the reader on a near-circular seven-mile route along the towpaths of central and north Oxford. Drawing on archive records and oral histories, *A Towpath Walk in Oxford* describes notable events and landmarks, and tells the stories of the characters – resourceful, eccentric, or notorious – who have shaped the varied waterway scene that Oxford enjoys today.

Includes detailed sections on Godstow, Port Meadow, Binsey, Medley, and Jericho.

'A remarkable compendium of historical fact and fiction concerning Oxford's waterways. It is equally readable as a practical walk guide or as a history book.' *Canal Boat & Inland Waterways magazine*

'At times like a pilgrimage, at times like a historical pub crawl … the perfect combination.' *Oxford Times Limited Edition magazine*

'A most informative text which never loses sight of the human element … a very easy read despite being choc-full with facts and details.' *Canal & Riverboat magazine*

'The whole book reads superbly.' William Horwood, Oxford author

'Beautifully done, a model of its kind.' Margaret Drabble, novelist and critic

Oxford Towpath Press ISBN 978-0-9535593-4-3
www.oxfordwaterwalks.co.uk

"KING OF ALL BALLOONS":

The Adventurous Life of James Sadler, First English Aeronaut

MARK DAVIES

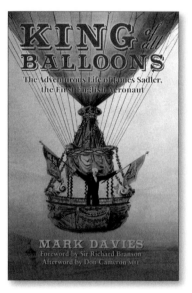

A pastry cook by trade, James Sadler of Oxford defied the constraints of his upbringing to achieve remarkable success not only as an 18th-century pioneer of hot-air ballooning but also as an inventor, notably of engines, guns, and cannon, and as Chemist to the Royal Navy. This biography is an attempt to revive the memory of a forgotten British hero, and of his ill-fated balloonist son Windham, who between them made ascents from forty or so towns and cities in England, Scotland, and Ireland.

'A very readable and thoughtful account of an important inventor and adventurer.' *Aerospace* (**Royal Aeronautical Society**)

'Mark Davies has done the nation a service by reconstructing the life and achievements of the first English balloonist.' *Country Life*

'Davies's admirable aim is to redress history's disregard.'
Times Literary Supplement

'A fascinating read, cleverly reconstructed, with input from all kinds of sources.' *How it Works*

'Entertaining insight into the behaviour and mannerisms of those eventful days.' *Aviation Historian*

'With this book Oxford historian Mark Davies fills a void.'
Ballooning (**Balloon Federation of America**)

Amberley Books, Stroud.   ISBN 978-1-4456-5308-2